NEVER COOK SOBER

COOKBOOK

Published by Adams Media,
a division of F+W Media, Inc.
57 Littlefield Street,
Avon, MA 02322. U.S.A.
www.adamsmedia.com

ISBN 10: 1-4405-3266-4
ISBN 13: 978-1-4405-3266-5
eISBN 10: 1-4405-3269-9
eISBN 13: 978-1-4405-3269-6

Printed in the United States of America.

10 9 8 7 6 5 4 3 2 1

Library of Congress Cataloging-in-Publication Data
is available from the publisher.

Many of the designations used by manufacturers and sellers to distinguish their product are claimed as trademarks. Where those designations appear in this book and Adams Media was aware of a trademark claim, the designations have been printed with initial capital letters.

Caution:
Certain sections of the book deal with cooking activities which, if not properly performed, could result in serious injury. The consumption of alcohol may impair your ability to perform such activities, increasing the risk of such injury. The authors, Adams Media, and F+W Media, Inc., do not accept liability for any injury, loss, legal consequence, or incidental or consequential damage incurred by reliance on the information or advice provided in this book.

This book is available at quantity discounts for bulk purchases.
For information, please call 1-800-289-0963.

NEVER COOK SOBER

COOKBOOK

PLUS: The Best Booze for Every Intoxicating Meal

From Soused Scrambled Eggs
TO KAHLUA FUDGE BROWNIES,
100 (FOOL) PROOF RECIPES

Stacy Laabs & Sherri Field

Adamsmedia

Avon, Massachusetts

ACKNOWLEDGMENTS

Stacy Laabs: I would like to thank my parents, Barbara Laabs and Larris Laabs, for all their support and love. I would also like to thank Aunt Jim for her encouragement and my cousins DK and Michael for all the fun family memories of childhood; wish we could have had more time.

My loving, dear friends, words can never express the thanks I feel toward all of you. We all get to choose our second family and I couldn't ask for a better one! To Sherri Devereau, the smartest and craziest woman I know with a heart of gold—love ya, my friend! I also thank Mark Harp, for always being there and for inspiration; Joanna Kowalik, for fun; Dave Friedman, my fellow storyteller; Lisa Zeschke, for caring and laughter; Alecia Burnett, for your 100 percent belief I would make it and keeping me on track when I doubted; Moriah Burnett, for encouragement; Pamela Weeks, my counterpart in adventure and art; Sara Looney, for always holding faith; Mark Davidson, for always having my back; Vince Darago, the best teacher I could have, for telling me I can!; Matthew Earl Jones for encouragement in my writing; Chris Griscom (the Light Institute) for always holding the light; Erle Montaigu (Tai Chi World), for helping me when I needed it—wish I'd known you longer my friend, RIP; Lisa Morgan, for telling me to do what I loved; Christine Roll, Mary Poole, Jennifer Jones—for great high school memories! To everyone else whom I didn't get to mention, thanks for touching my life. Special thanks to Sherri Field—for everything.

Sherri Field: I would like to thank my parents Steve Field and Carol Field for all their love, support, and encouragement. I thank my sister, Kristina (Field) Graves for all those precious years of love and razzing. I have valued and enjoyed every moment. I would also like to thank my Aunt Terry and Uncle Ron for always being there; my cousins Craig, Chris, and Desiree for all the fun family memories; Melissa LaMancusa for her friendship over the years and being there during the good times and the rough times; Charlie Briggs for his adventurous nature, kindness, and encouragement; Shyla Yosten for her friendship and all the laughs. To everyone else who has touched my life, thank you! Special thanks to Stacy Laabs for showing me dreams can come true!

Stacy and Sherri would both like to thank the following people for all the contributions in getting the book accomplished!

Gina Panettieri—We appreciate you taking a chance! Here is to a great book!

Paula Munier—For giving us the opportunity and being a wonderful editor!

Meredith O'Hayre—Thank you for your support and guidance!

Jennifer Lawler—We appreciate your help and patience!

Adams Media—Thanks for the first shot!

Mark Pavlovich—For your years of believing and never giving up.

Ric Villa—Thank you for your support and insight. They are invaluable.

Dana Achten—For being one talented, terrific chef!

Matt Nunes—Drink Master and Bartender King!

Forrist Lytehaause—Marketing Brilliant Mind!

The pups—Savannah, Sydney, and D-Back.

To all the bartenders, cooks, partiers, and great musicians who make great memories for a lifetime!

CONTENTS

CHAPTER 3: Dinner   **69**

CHAPTER 4: Desserts   105

INTRODUCTION

There's nothing quite like having a glass of wine with dinner. Or while you're cooking dinner. Or, in fact, *in* your dinner. The same is true of beer, vodka, rum, tequila—you name it. If it has alcohol in it, it can spice up your meal times.

That's where this cookbook comes in. You'll find recipes for drinks and for meals—from breakfast to dessert, from a Bottoms-Up Mudslide Smoothie (Chapter 1) to Wasted Beer Beef Stew (Chapter 3). We say fix a drink or two, kick your feet up, survey the menu of life and indulge! The goal is for you to be able to relax and enjoy cooking (and eating) no matter when or why: after a hard day at work, or while enjoying a night in with friends, or while spicing up a relationship, or even when you're all alone. It's all about *your* attitude!

Getting Started

Everyone has different cocktail, wine, and beer preferences. Use these recipes as guides to inspire you! Find great taste that fits you in every day of your life!

- One thing we recommend to keep your cost down is miniature bottles of alcohol, also known as minis, nips, shooters, or airplane bottles. This practice will allow you to purchase a variety of alcohols to make these great-tasting recipes without inflicting too much pain on your wallet. You can find miniature bottles of alcohol at your local liquor or grocery store.
- Play with the flavors and the alcohol content. People prefer different amounts of spice or alcohol in a dish. Depending on how tipsy you are, that might change the taste of a dish as well!
- Take a moment to focus and celebrate the "raise your glass" toasts. They are included as a reminder that life is to be enjoyed and to always remain surprised by life's gifts that can come at any time!

Shots

There is some debate in the alcohol world about how many ounces are in a shot. Depending on the shot glass, the volume it holds can be anywhere from 1 to 3 ounces. Shots in the recipes for this book are based on this ratio: 1 shot equals 1½ ounces or 3 tablespoons.

In each recipe, an alcohol content is listed, with 1–6 icons representing the various amounts in each recipe. These tables show how much alcohol each icon represents.

Hard Liquor Content Chart

Measurement	Equivalents	# of Shots	Icons
up to 1½ ounces	3 tablespoons or less	1 shot or less	1
1½ to 3 ounces	3–6 tablespoons	1–2 shots	2
3 to 4½ ounces	6–9 tablespoons	2-3 shots	3
4½ to 6 ounces	9–12 tablespoons	3–4 shots	4
6 to 7½ ounces	12–15 tablespoons	4–5 shots	5
7½ ounces and above	15 tablespoons or more	5 or more shots	6

Wine Measurements

Measurement	Equivalents	Icons
up to ¼ cup	up to 5 tablespoons	1
¼ to ½ cup	5–10 tablespoons	2
½ to ¾ cup	10–15 tablespoons	3
¾ to 1 cup	15–20 tablespoons	4
1 to 2 cups	20 tablespoons or more	5

Beer

Measurement	Equivalents	Icons
¼ cup	n/a	1
½ cup	n/a	2
1½ cups	1 bottle beer	3
3 cups	2 bottles beer	4

Go drink, eat, and drink some more and salute to all your dreams, forgive your mistakes, and move on to embracing your goals on the journey. Remember, it's all about finding fun in the hard times, living life like you have all the time in the world, and laughing like crazy. Life is too short, so carpe diem!

CHAPTER 1

Breakfast

Breakfast sets the tone for your day. Will today be one of those corporate-drone days where you down a cup of instant alertness while slurping some reconstituted oatmeal? Or, will today be a fun day, an adventuresome day, perhaps a "sick" day? If that's the case, then toss your oatmeal packet aside and replace your instant alertness with some instant light-heartedness.

In this chapter, you'll find energizing recipes that will give your day the kick-start it needs. Whether you want the virtue of yogurt, the rib-sticking satisfaction of scrambled eggs, or the chocolate decadence of a morning Bottoms-Up Mudslide Smoothie, you'll find a breakfast to make your day.

Three Sheets to the Wind Vodka and Rum Fruit Plate

There are better things in life than alcohol, but alcohol makes up for not having them.
—TERRY PRATCHETT

SERVES 6–12

- 1–2 bananas, sliced and spritzed with lemon
- 1–2 red apples, sliced and spritzed with lemon
- 1 package of strawberries, sliced or whole
- 1–2 oranges, sliced and peeled
- 1–2 pineapples, sliced and peeled
- 1 green apple, sliced, peeled and spritzed with lemon
- 1 shot glass blueberry/pomegranate vodka
- 1 shot glass 360 Double Chocolate vodka
- 1 shot glass raspberry vodka
- 1 shot glass cherry rum
- 1 shot glass passion fruit rum
- 1 shot glass melon rum

1. Slice your fruit. Decide how you want to feast and put each fruit on its own plate or place them all together on one platter.
2. Place shots of liquor in shot glasses or small bowls. (If you don't have six shot glasses, it's time to start collecting them.)
3. Dip fruit into the shot glasses with toothpicks or use a spoon to lightly sprinkle the alcohol on the fruits. Enjoy!

ALCOHOL CONTENT:

SUGGESTED PAIRING: **Bananas with 360 Double Chocolate Vodka**
Red apples with blueberry/pomegranate vodka
Strawberries with cherry rum
Orange with raspberry vodka
Pineapple with passion fruit rum
Green apples with melon rum

Drink pairing: *Mai Tai*	
1 ounce light rum 1 ounce dark rum 1 ounce triple sec ½ ounce grenadine 1 ounce lime juice 4 ounces orange juice 4 ounces pineapple juice 1 cherry, for garnish 1 pineapple wedge, for garnish	Pour all ingredients (except the garnishes) into a shaker. Shake well to mix. Pour mixture through a strainer into a tall glass. Garnish with the cherry and the pineapple wedge.

May you live all the years of your life. **Jonathan Swift**

Hazy Tequila-Salsa Scrambled Eggs

Is the glass half full, or half empty? It depends on whether you're pouring, or drinking.
—BILL COSBY

SERVES 1

2 eggs

1 tablespoon green chilies

Pinch of salt

½ shot tequila

1 tablespoon butter

1 tablespoon salsa (your favorite) or to taste

1. Mix eggs, chilies, salt, and tequila in bowl.
2. In a pan, melt butter over low heat. Pour egg mixture into the pan. Cook over medium-low heat, stirring eggs occasionally until they are cooked to the desired consistency. Top with salsa.

ALCOHOL CONTENT:

Drink Pairing: *Tequila Sunrise*	
1–2 cups ice 2 ounces tequila 4 ounces orange juice ½ ounce grenadine 1 orange slice (optional) 1 maraschino cherry (optional)	Fill a highball glass with ice. Pour the tequila and the orange juice over the ice. Stir. Slowly pour the grenadine around the inside edge of the glass. The grenadine should go straight to the bottom and then rise up slowly through the drink. Garnish with the orange slice and cherry.

I am not old, but mellow, like good wine. **Stephen Phillips**

Tipsy Trivia

"It's for medicinal purposes." Tequila is made from the agave plant—a plant so powerful that the Aztecs once reserved it for priests, nobility, and the very ill, according to *The Complete Book of Spirits: A Guide to Their History, Production, and Enjoyment* by Anthony Dias Blue.

Raise Your Glass to Great Health!

Giddy Raspberry Tea Vodka Granola Yogurt

I like to do most anything; play with animals, mostly. And vodka's kind of a hobby.
—**BETTY WHITE**

SERVES 1

4 ounces vanilla yogurt

⅓ cup granola

½ teaspoon raspberry tea vodka or to taste

Kosher salt, few grains

1. Combine yogurt, granola, raspberry tea vodka, and salt in a bowl. (If only all recipes were this easy!)

ALCOHOL CONTENT:

Drink pairing: *Sea Breeze*	
1–2 cups ice 1½ ounces vodka 4 ounces fresh grapefruit juice 1½ ounces cranberry juice 1 lime wedge, for garnish	Fill a highball (or other tall) glass with ice. Pour in vodka, grapefruit juice, and cranberry juice. Garnish with a lime wedge.

May you get all your wishes but one, so you always have something to strive for! **Irish drinking toast**

Tipsy Trivia
Vodka's clarity and clean taste allows it to hide in a punch bowl, where it has been known to surprise the occasional new drinker.

Raise Your Glass to Your Dreams!

Distracted Bourbon Pecan Waffles

A drink a day keeps the shrink away.
—EDWARD ABBEY

SERVES 6

1 cup all-purpose flour

2 teaspoons baking powder

½ teaspoon salt

2 eggs, separated

1 cup buttermilk

1 shot bourbon

1 teaspoon vanilla extract

3 tablespoons melted butter

½ cup chopped pecans

Maple syrup (optional)

1. In a bowl, combine flour, baking powder, and salt.
2. In a separate bowl, mix egg yolks, buttermilk, bourbon, vanilla, butter, and pecans.
3. Blend wet mixture into dry mixture. Beat until smooth.
4. Use a mixer to beat egg whites until they are stiff. Fold egg whites into the batter.
5. Fill waffle iron with batter and cook according to waffle iron directions until the waffles are a lovely bourbon color! Remove and place on plate, then add whatever syrup rocks your world.

ALCOHOL CONTENT:

Drink pairing: *A Kiss Goodnight*	
1½ ounces strawberry vodka 1½ ounces Sour Raspberry Pucker 3–4 ounces cranberry juice 3–4 ounces 7UP 1 splash rum, dark	Pour strawberry vodka and Sour Raspberry Pucker into a highball glass. Add the cranberry juice, then an equal amount of 7UP. Float a splash of dark rum on top.

To get the full value of joy, you must have someone to divide it with.
Mark Twain

Tipsy Trivia
Praise the Lord! Bourbon was invented by a Baptist minister named Elijah Craig.

Tanked Cinnamon Whiskey and Brown Sugar Oatmeal

The telephone is a good way to talk to people without having to offer them a drink.

—FRAN LEBOWITZ

SERVES 1

½ cup oatmeal

½ cup water

½ cup milk (regular, rice, soy, or almond)

1½ tablespoons cinnamon whiskey, divided

1½ tablespoons brown sugar, divided

Few grains kosher salt

½ teaspoon salted butter

2 tablespoons walnuts, roasted

1. In a small saucepan, mix oatmeal, water, and milk together. Bring to a boil. Add 1 tablespoon cinnamon whiskey, 1 tablespoon brown sugar, and salt. Reduce heat to medium and cook to the consistency of Thanksgiving stuffing.

2. When ready to serve, stir in the remaining ½ tablespoon cinnamon whiskey, ½ tablespoon brown sugar, and butter. Sprinkle with walnuts.

ALCOHOL CONTENT:

Drink Pairing: *Spanish Coffee*	
½ ounce coffee liqueur ½ ounce rum 1 cup of brewed coffee 1½ ounces whipped cream 1 cherry (optional)	Add liqueur, rum, and coffee to the coffee mug. Top with whipped cream. Garnish with a cherry.

May misfortune follow you the rest of your life, but never catch up. **Irish drinking toast**

> **Tipsy Trivia**
> The difference in bourbon flavors comes from the grain selections in the mash. Bourbon must use at least 51 percent corn in its mash to be called "bourbon," though most use 60 percent to 80 percent corn.

Lit Banana Rum Pancakes

The road to excess leads to the palace of wisdom.
—WILLIAM BLAKE

SERVES 2

1½ cups all-purpose flour

1½ teaspoons baking powder

¾ teaspoon salt

3 tablespoons sugar

2 large eggs

1½ cups buttermilk

3 tablespoons unsalted butter, melted

½ teaspoon vanilla extract

Banana Rum Sauce

2 tablespoons butter

2 tablespoons brown sugar

¼ teaspoon cinnamon

2 bananas, sliced and spritzed with lemon

2 shots dark rum

Pinch of salt

1. Mix flour, baking powder, salt, and sugar in a bowl. Set aside.
2. In a separate bowl, beat eggs. Add buttermilk, melted butter, and vanilla.
3. Add the dry ingredients to the wet ingredients and stir until mixed. Some lumps are okay. Let the batter rest for a few minutes prior to cooking.
4. Drop batter by the spoonful onto a hot, greased griddle or in a pan over medium heat on the stove. Flip pancake when batter rises and bubbles appear. Continue to cook until light brown. Serve with Banana Rum Sauce.

Banana Rum Sauce

1. In a pan, melt butter over low heat. Add sugar, cinnamon, bananas, rum, and salt. Cook slowly until sauce is warm and bananas have softened. Pour over pancakes. Be generous with the sauce. It's the best part!

ALCOHOL CONTENT:

Drink Pairing: *Cuda (Barracuda)*	
1½ ounces rum, 151 proof 1½ ounces vodka 1½ ounces grenadine 1½ ounces lime juice 1–2 cups ice	Fill a shaker with ice. Add all ingredients. Mix. Strain into a highball glass filled with ice.

May your neighbors respect you, trouble neglect you, the angels protect you, and heaven accept you! **Irish toast**

> **Tipsy Trivia**
> Baking powder is made from cream of tartar, and cream of tartar can only be found on the sides of wooden wine casks. So the next time you eat a scone, thank a vintner.

Temptation Bourbon Vanilla French Toast

There can't be good living where there is not good drinking.

—BENJAMIN FRANKLIN

SERVES 6

3 eggs

¾ cup milk

1½ teaspoons vanilla extract

½ teaspoon ground cinnamon

1 shot bourbon

Pinch of salt

6 slices French bread, cut thick

Few tablespoons butter, divided

Maple syrup, to taste

1. In a bowl, mix together eggs, milk, vanilla, cinnamon, bourbon, and salt. Pour this batter into a shallow dish.
2. Heat griddle on medium heat. Add 1 tablespoon or more of butter to griddle, allowing it to melt. Place a bread slice in the batter, fully coating both sides. Place bread slice on griddle. Repeat with as many slices as you can fit on the griddle. Cook until slices are brown on both sides.
3. Repeat until all slices are cooked. Top with butter and maple syrup.

ALCOHOL CONTENT:

Drink Pairing: *Café Brûlot* **(aka, *Impress Your Friends with a Flaming Drink*)**	
3 sticks cinnamon, broken 6 whole cloves 4 sugar cubes or 4 teaspoons sugar 1 long strip orange peel, cleaned 1 long strip lemon peel, cleaned ½ cup brandy 2 cups hot, very strong brewed coffee	1. In a double boiler combine cinnamon, cloves, sugar, orange peel, and lemon peel. 2. Heat brandy in a small saucepan until it's hot but not boiling. Remove from heat and set on fire using a match (this is the part where you amaze your friends). 3. When the flames have gone out, pour the brandy over the mixture in the double boiler. Stir in coffee. 4. Strain out the cinnamon pieces, cloves, and peels before serving. Makes 4 4-ounce servings.

Always remember to forget the troubles that passed away, but never forget to remember the blessings that come each day. **Traditional toast**

> **Tipsy Trivia**
> **Frederick the Great of Prussia tried to implement coffee prohibition. He wanted people to drink alcohol instead.**

Morning After Mango Rum Breakfast Burrito

A rum and Pepsi is just not the same as a rum and Coke.
—BILLY BOB THORNTON

SERVES 2

1 tablespoon butter

1 tablespoon olive oil

¼ cup onions, diced

½ medium-sized tomato, diced

1 cup ham, cubed

4 eggs

½ shot mango rum

Pinch of salt

4 flour tortillas

1 cup grated Cheddar cheese or to taste

½ cup salsa or to taste

1. Add butter and olive oil to a pan over medium heat. When butter is melted, add onions, tomato, and ham. Cook until onions are clear and ham is heated.
2. Whisk eggs in a small bowl with mango rum and salt. Pour into pan. Reduce heat to low and scramble until eggs reach desired consistency.
3. Spoon eggs across middle of tortillas. Add cheese and salsa. Roll the tortilla up burrito-style. Cut in half and serve.

ALCOHOL CONTENT:

Drink pairing: *Orange Margarita*	
Ice 1 ounce tequila ½ ounce triple sec 4–6 ounces orange juice 1 splash lime juice or sour mix	Fill a margarita glass with ice. Add tequila, triple sec, and orange juice. Pour in a splash of lime juice or sour mix, and serve.

Here's to high walls and deep moats in the Zombie Apocalypse. **Zombie Hunters' Creed**

Tipsy Trivia

A Los Angeles bootlegger was acquitted in 1928 when the jury drank all the evidence. The jurors claimed to be testing whether the evidence really contained alcohol. It did, and then it was the jury's turn to go on trial.

Raise Your Glass to Playfulness!

Soused Scrambled Eggs with Champagne and Smoked Salmon

Why do I drink champagne for breakfast? Doesn't everyone?
—NOEL COWARD

SERVES 2

2 teaspoons butter

2 teaspoons olive oil

2 slices smoked salmon

4 large eggs (2 eggs per person)

1 teaspoon chives, finely chopped

¼ cup champagne

½ cup heavy cream

Salt and pepper to taste

1. In a nonstick pan over medium heat, melt butter with olive oil. When hot, heat the salmon slices until warm. Remove them from the pan and keep them warm.
2. In a bowl, whisk together the eggs, chives, champagne, heavy cream, salt, and pepper and whisk until just combined.
3. Add egg mixture to the pan. Scramble eggs using a plastic or wooden spoon until the eggs are cooked to the desired texture. Pour over salmon slices and serve.

ALCOHOL CONTENT:

Drink Pairing: *Champagne*

Here's champagne to our real friends, and real pain to our sham friends!
Author unknown

Tipsy Trivia
High-quality champagne has tiny bubbles while low-quality champagne has large bubbles. A mug of champagne with a head is probably actually a beer.

Raise Your Glass to Prosperity!

Loaded Oatmeal

Drinking wine was not a snobbism nor a sign of sophistication nor a cult; it was as natural as eating and to me as necessary.

—ERNEST HEMINGWAY

SERVES 1

½ cup oatmeal

½ cup water

½ cup milk (plain, rice, soy, or almond)

Few grains kosher salt

3 tablespoons cinnamon whiskey, divided

3 tablespoons raspberry vodka, divided

1½ tablespoons brown sugar

½ teaspoon salted butter

1½ tablespoons almonds, toasted

1. In a small, dry saucepan, toast the oatmeal over low heat until a nutty aroma is produced.
2. Stir in water, milk, and salt. Bring to a boil. Add 1 tablespoon cinnamon whiskey and 1 tablespoon raspberry vodka. Stir oatmeal mixture until desired consistency is reached.
3. When ready to serve, stir in remaining 2 tablespoons cinnamon whiskey, remaining 2 tablespoons raspberry vodka, brown sugar, butter, and almonds.

ALCOHOL CONTENT:

Drink pairing: *Hypnotic Colada*	
1 ounce Hpnotiq ½ ounce raspberry vodka 2 ounces coconut liqueur 2 ounces cranberry juice 2 ounces pineapple juice 1 splash grenadine 1–2 cups ice 1 pineapple slice (optional)	Blend ingredients with enough ice to fill a hurricane glass. Pour into the hurricane glass. Toss in a splash of grenadine for color. Garnish with a pineapple slice, if desired.

To all the days here and after. May they be filled with fond memories, happiness, and laughter. **Traditional toast**

Tipsy Trivia

A hurricane glass is a tall, fluted glass commonly used for blended cocktails. We call it a hurricane glass because it looks like a hurricane lamp, which could keep your flame alive despite the wind.

Pick-Me-Up Rum Fruit Smoothie

You moon the wrong person at an office party and suddenly you're not "professional" anymore.

—JEFF FOXWORTHY

SERVES 2

1 cup orange juice

¼ cup vanilla yogurt

1 banana

1 cup strawberries

1 shot rum

1 cup ice

Pinch of salt

1. Combine all ingredients in a blender. Blend until smooth and serve.

ALCOHOL CONTENT:

Drink pairing: *Shot of rum, of course!*

May you always have a cool head and a warm heart. **Traditional toast**

Tipsy Trivia

In Fairbanks, Alaska, it is illegal to serve alcoholic beverages to a moose—though it is legal to accept a drink from a moose.

Raise Your Glass to Creativity!

Jiggling Vodka Shots

Once we hit forty, women only have about four taste buds left: one for vodka, one for wine, one for cheese, and one for chocolate.

—GINA BARRECA

SERVES 10

1 package flavored gelatin (6 ounces)
16 ounces boiling water
6 ounces cold water
10 ounces cheap vodka

1. Make the gelatin according to the package instructions using the boiling water. Add the cold water and vodka. Pour the gelatin into shot glasses and refrigerate. Serve when solid.

ALCOHOL CONTENT:

Drink pairing: *Greek Coffee*	
1½ ounces ouzo 6 ounces brewed coffee 1½ ounces whipped cream 1 black licorice stick (optional)	Pour the ouzo and coffee into a coffee cup. Top with whipped cream. Garnish with a black licorice stick as a stirrer.

May the best day of your past be the worst day of your future.
Traditional toast

> **Tipsy Trivia**
> Anise liqueur can only be called "ouzo" if it is made in Greece. Most ouzo is made on the island of Lesbos.

Raise Your Glass to Inspiration!

Seeing Double Frangelico French Toast

I never drink water because of the disgusting things that fish do in it.

—W. C. FIELDS

SERVES 6

3 eggs

¾ cup milk

1½ teaspoons vanilla extract

½ teaspoon ground cinnamon

1 shot Frangelico

Pinch of salt

6 thick slices of french bread

Few tablespoons butter, divided

Maple syrup (optional)

1. In a bowl, mix together eggs, milk, vanilla, cinnamon, Frangelico, and salt. Pour into shallow dish.
2. Heat griddle on medium heat. Add 1 tablespoon butter to griddle and melt. Place 1 slice of bread in batter, then flip to ensure both sides are fully coated. Place bread slice on buttered griddle. Continue with bread slices until griddle is full.
3. Cook until brown on both sides.
4. Continue cooking bread slices until all are cooked. Top with butter and warmed maple syrup.

ALCOHOL CONTENT:

Drink pairing: *Blood Orange Mimosa*	
4 ounces blood orange juice 4 ounces champagne or prosecco (or other dry white wine) 1 blood orange slice (optional)	Fill a champagne flute halfway with blood orange juice. Top with champagne or prosecco and garnish with an orange slice, if desired.

May your bank account always be bigger than your troubles. **Author unknown**

> **Tipsy Trivia**
> **Frangelico is a hazelnut liqueur, invented 300 years ago by Italian monks. It was invented in the Piedmont region of northern Italy and is still produced there.**

Intoxicated Tequila Breakfast Tacos

So I was drinking tequila, and I was drinking grappa, which is Italian for "gasoline," and I was drinking Jägermeister, which I believe is the liquid equivalent of Wonder Woman's golden lasso, because it will make you tell anybody the truth for no reason whatsoever. . . "You have really bad skin. Thanks for the drink."

—**MARGARET CHO**

SERVES 4

5 ounces chorizo sausage

1 cup refried beans

4 eggs

½ shot tequila

Pinch of salt

4 flour or corn tortillas

1 cup any shredded cheese (optional)

¼ cup salsa (optional)

1. Cook chorizo sausage in a pan over medium-high heat until brown. Drain on paper towels and set aside. Reserve pan and drippings for later use.
2. Heat refried beans in a small saucepan over medium heat. Set aside.
3. Whisk eggs, tequila, and salt in a small bowl. Pour into pan used for frying chorizo. Cook over medium heat until eggs reach desired consistency.
4. Spread refried beans on the tortillas. Spoon cooked eggs across the center of the refried beans. Add cheese and your favorite salsa. Roll up the tortillas and serve.

ALCOHOL CONTENT:

Drink pairing: *Bloody Maria*	
1 ounce tequila 2 ounces tomato juice 1 dash lemon juice 1 dash hot sauce 1 dash celery salt 1 glass of ice cubes 1 lemon or lime wedge, for garnish 1 celery stalk, for garnish	Fill a highball glass with ice cubes. Add all ingredients except garnishes. If you have someone to impress, mix by pouring from one glass to another a few times. Otherwise use a stirrer or a spoon. Garnish with lemon, lime, and/or celery according to your preferences.

> **Tipsy Trivia**
> The Lepcha people of Tibet pay their teachers with alcohol, which is a little like paying football players with Advil.

My friends are the best friends—loyal, willing and able. Now let's get to drinking! All glasses off the table! **Traditional toast**

Bottoms-Up Mudslide Smoothie

Spring is nature's way of saying, "Let's party!"

—ROBIN WILLIAMS

SERVES 2

2 cups ice

½ cup half and half

1 shot espresso

1 shot vodka

1 shot Irish cream

1 shot Kahlua

Pinch of salt

2–3 tablespoons chocolate syrup, to taste

Whipped cream, for garnish

1. Blend ice, half and half, espresso, vodka, Irish cream, Kahlua, and salt in blender.
2. Coat the inside of 2 glasses with a thin layer of chocolate syrup. Pour the smoothie into the chocolate-coated glasses. Top with whipped cream and serve.

ALCOHOL CONTENT:

Drink pairing: *Mocha Shot*	
¾ ounce white crème de cacao ¾ ounce Kahlua	Fill a shot glass halfway with crème de cacao. Float remainder of glass with Kahlua.

Here's to a long life and a merry one. A quick death and an easy one. A pretty girl and an honest one. A cold pint—and another one! **Irish toast**

Barmaid Mango Rum Cream Cheese Bagels

I try not to drink too much because when I'm drunk, I bite.
—BETTE MIDLER

SERVES 2

2 bagels
½ teaspoon of mango rum
¼ cup of plain cream cheese
Pinch of salt

1. Toast bagel if desired. In a small bowl mix the cream cheese, mango rum, and salt. Spread over bagel and enjoy.

ALCOHOL CONTENT:

Drink pairing: *West Indian Colada*	
½ fresh papaya, peeled and diced 1⅔ ounces white rum ⅔ ounce coconut rum 2 ounces pineapple juice ⅔ ounce coconut cream 1 ounce heavy cream 1 cup crushed ice 1 pineapple wedge, for garnish	Place diced papaya in an electric blender. Add rums, pineapple juice, creams, and ice. Blend until smooth. Pour blender contents into a chilled piña colada glass. Garnish with the fresh pineapple wedge.

Here's to a temperance supper, with water in glasses tall, and coffee and tea to end with—And me not there at all! **Irish toast**

> **Tipsy Trivia**
> The Hebrew toast *l'chaim!* means "to life!" Hebrew letters are also numbers and the first letter in "chaim" is associated with the number eighteen. This is why Jewish people often give gifts and donations in multiples of eighteen.

Raise Your Glass to Entertaining!

Double Blueberry Vodka Muffins

I believe if life gives you lemons, make lemonade . . . then find someone that life gave vodka to and have a party.

—RON WHITE

SERVES 6–8

¼ cup butter, slightly softened

½ cup sugar

1 egg

¼ cup milk

1 cup flour

1 teaspoon baking powder

¼ teaspoon salt

½ teaspoon cinnamon

1 cup fresh or frozen blueberries

½ teaspoon blueberry vodka per muffin

1. Preheat oven to 375°F.
2. Cream butter and sugar together in a bowl.
3. Beat the egg and add it to the mixture. Add milk and stir.
4. In a separate bowl, mix dry ingredients together (not including blueberries). Add to the wet ingredients. Mix together until combined. Add blueberries and stir gently.
5. Place a paper liner in each muffin tin. Put a small amount of batter in the bottom of each cup and add ½ teaspoon of blueberry vodka. Add batter on top of vodka until cups are about ⅔ full. Gently mix the batter and vodka together. Bake for 20 minutes or until golden brown. Enjoy!

ALCOHOL CONTENT:

Drink pairing: *Cape Breeze*	
1–2 cups ice 1½ ounces coconut flavored rum 2 ounces cranberry juice 2 ounces grapefruit juice ½ teaspoon superfine sugar (you can make superfine sugar by putting regular sugar in a blender or food processor and grinding until powdery.)	Place ice in a highball glass. Add coconut rum, cranberry juice, grapefruit juice, and sugar. Stir.

Here's to being single . . . drinking doubles . . . and seeing triple!
Various attributions

> **Tipsy Trivia**
> About half of the alcohol in a baking recipe is burned off in 25 minutes. So does that make these muffins half empty or half full?

Caribbean Cocktail Rum Jelly and Toast

Remember, your body needs 6 to 8 glasses of fluid daily. Straight up or on the rocks.
—**P. J. O'ROURKE**

SERVES 1

1 slice bread

1 tablespoon strawberry jelly

½ teaspoon strawberry rum

1. Toast bread. In a small bowl, combine jelly with strawberry rum. Spread the jelly on the toast and enjoy!

ALCOHOL CONTENT:

Drink pairing: *Big Hug*	
1 ounce crème de cacao 6 ounces hot chocolate ½ ounce Irish cream	In a mug, add crème de cacao and hot chocolate. Pour the Irish cream over the back of a spoon to float it on the top, creating a layered drink.

I drink to your health when I'm with you, I drink to your health when I'm alone, I drink to your health so often, I'm starting to worry about my own! **Various attributions**

> **Tipsy Trivia**
> Other layered drinks include the B-52, the Oatmeal Cookie, and the Slippery Nipple.

Raise Your Glass to Vacations!

CHAPTER 2

Lunch

Hearken back to the golden days of the three-martini lunch, when people knew how to wash away the insanity of the morning and fortify themselves for the hours ahead. The problem is, once you've headed out and started discussing life with your favorite bartender, you might not have the willpower that it takes to get back to the grind.

So we've created a midday happy hour with recipes that lift the spirit, smooth the hackles, and relax the soul. At least until that first afternoon meeting.

In this chapter you will find salads and pastas, hot dogs and chili, and oysters and mussels. Between them you'll find the perfect meal to launch yourself into your afternoon.

Wobbly Chicken Tequila Fettuccine

I don't go out with my single friends—not at all—because I never have a good time, never have fun. We go to a club, a guy comes over: "Hey, can I buy you a drink?" They're like, "No, she's married." I'm like, "Yeah, I'm married, but I'm thirsty. Why don't you shut the hell up, and let me have a free drink?"

—WANDA SYKES

SERVES 4

3 tablespoons butter, divided

1½ tablespoons minced garlic

⅓ cup chopped fresh cilantro, divided

2 tablespoons minced jalapeño peppers

1½ shots tequila

2 tablespoons fresh lime juice

2 quarts chicken stock, divided

3 tablespoons soy sauce

1 pound boneless, skinless chicken breast, cubed

1 package fettuccine pasta (16 ounces)

¼ red onion, sliced

1½ cups bell pepper, multicolored, thinly sliced

1 tablespoon olive oil

1½ cups heavy whipping cream

Tipsy Trivia
The worm in tequila is an ancient tradition dating back to 1950 when Jacobo Lozano Paez started putting them into bottles of mescal. This was either a stroke of marketing genius, or an experiment to see if he could get gringos to eat worms.

1. In a saucepan over medium heat, add 2 tablespoons of butter, garlic, most of the cilantro (leave a little for garnish), and jalapeño. Sauté for 3 minutes.
2. Mix in tequila, lime juice, and ⅓ cup chicken stock and bring to a boil. Let the sauce thicken and set aside.
3. In a small bowl, drizzle soy sauce over chicken and set aside.
4. In a large saucepan, boil the remaining chicken stock. Add pasta and cook to desired doneness following package directions. Drain and set aside.
5. In a medium-sized pan, sauté onion and multicolored bell peppers with the olive oil and remaining tablespoon of butter. Stir occasionally until onions are soft and clear. Toss in chicken, sauce, and whipping cream. Bring to a boil, then reduce heat and simmer until chicken is cooked completely. Serve over the pasta and sprinkle cilantro on top for garnish.

ALCOHOL CONTENT:

SUGGESTED PAIRING: Asparagus

Drink Pairing: *Chardonnay*

Here's to health, peace, and prosperity. May the flower of love never be nipped by the frost of disappointment, nor shadow of grief fall among your family and friends. **Irish toast**

Under the Table Vodka Chicken Salad

A man is a fool if he drinks before he reaches the age of fifty, and a fool if he doesn't afterward.
—**FRANK LLOYD WRIGHT**

SERVES 4

1 cup chicken, cooked

1 package fresh spinach

1 stalk celery, sliced

1 green onion, sliced

½ cucumber, sliced

1 carrot, sliced

¼ cup ranch dressing

½ shot cucumber vodka

Pinch of sugar

Few salt grains

Ground black pepper, to taste

1. In a bowl, mix together the chicken, spinach, and sliced vegetables to create a salad. Set aside.
2. In a second bowl, pour in ranch dressing, then add cucumber vodka, sugar, salt, and black pepper. Mix well.
3. Drizzle the dressing over the chicken and enjoy!

ALCOHOL CONTENT:

SUGGESTED PAIRING: Croissant

Drink Pairing: *Cucumber Martini*	
2 thin cucumber slices, divided Few mint leaves, divided 2 ounces gin 2 teaspoons dry vermouth 1 glass ice cubes	1. Muddle (crush ingredients in the bottom of a glass to make them more flavorful) one of the cucumber slices and all but one of the mint leaves in a cocktail shaker. Add gin, vermouth, and ice. Shake until mixed. 2. Strain shaker contents into a chilled martini glass. Garnish with the remaining cucumber slice and/or mint leaf.

May your home always be too small to hold all your friends. **Traditional toast**

Tipsy Trivia
The Russian word for "water" is "vodka."

Plastered Vodka Turkey Wrap

Stay busy, get plenty of exercise, and don't drink too much. Then again, don't drink too little.
—HERMAN "JACKRABBIT" SMITH-JOHANNSEN

SERVES 1

2 tablespoons Dijon mustard

1 teaspoon vodka

1 spinach or tomato-basil tortilla

2 romaine lettuce leaves

2 slices tomato

1 slice Cheddar cheese

2 ounces turkey, sliced

Salt and pepper to taste

1. Mix Dijon mustard and vodka together. Spread on tortilla. Add lettuce, tomato, cheese, turkey, salt, and pepper.
2. Roll tightly and cut diagonally in half. Enjoy!

ALCOHOL CONTENT:

SUGGESTED PAIRING: Potato chips

Drink Pairing: *Devastating Body Rocker*	
1 part blackberry brandy 1 part gin	In a shot glass, combine ingredients. Voilà! That was easy.

May the roof above you never fall in and those gathered beneath it never fall out. **Traditional toast**

> **Tipsy Trivia**
> Swedes distilled vodka to make gunpowder in the fifteenth century. We hear they had a blast.

Caramelized Red Wine Onions and Mushroom Burger

Wine is a living liquid containing no preservatives. Its life cycle comprises youth, maturity, old age, and death. When not treated with reasonable respect it will sicken and die.

—JULIA CHILD

SERVES 4

Caramelized Red Wine Onions

1 medium-sized sweet onion

1 tablespoon olive oil

½ cup red wine

Salt and pepper to taste

Mushroom Burger Patties

1 pound ground beef

1 teaspoon salt

1 4-ounce can sliced mushrooms, drained

¼ tablespoon Worcestershire sauce

¼ cup chopped onion

1 teaspoon olive oil

1 lettuce leaf

2 slices tomato

1. Slice onion into thin rings. Add oil to pan and heat on medium. Let cook, stirring occasionally, until onions are golden brown.
2. Add wine, salt and pepper. Continue cooking onions until most of the wine has evaporated. Set aside.
3. In a bowl, combine beef, salt, mushrooms, Worcestershire, chopped onion, and oil. Form hamburger patties. Grill until desired doneness.
4. Serve on bun, with lettuce, tomato, and caramelized onions.

ALCOHOL CONTENT:

SUGGESTED PAIRING: Pasta salad

Drink Pairing: *Brown Ale Beer*

When wine enlivens the heart, may friendship surround the table.
Oliver Wendell Holmes

> ### Tipsy Trivia
> **Young wine is said to have an aroma, while mature wine is said to have a bouquet. It is best to avoid a wine with a "smell."**

Tipsy Tequila Lime Chicken Tacos

One tequila, two tequila, three tequila, floor.
—GEORGE CARLIN

SERVES 2

1 tablespoon olive oil

2 boneless, skinless chicken breasts, cooked and shredded, or cubed

¼ cup fresh lime juice

1 shot tequila

½ shot triple sec

¼ teaspoon red pepper flakes

½ teaspoon salt

½ teaspoon sugar

1 clove garlic, smashed

4 corn tortillas

Salsa, for garnish

Sour cream, for garnish

Cilantro, for garnish

1. Heat a frying pan with olive oil on medium and add chicken till warmed. Add lime juice, tequila, triple sec, red pepper flakes, salt, sugar, and garlic. Simmer for approximately 10 minutes, stirring occasionally.
2. Warm tortillas in the microwave and add the chicken. Garnish with other fixings on top as desired.

ALCOHOL CONTENT:

SUGGESTED PAIRING: Black beans

Drink pairing: *Margarita*	
Salt or sugar to rim the glass (optional) 1–2 cups ice cubes 1½ ounces tequila ½ ounce triple sec 3 ounces sour mix Lime wedge (optional) Dash of lemon or lime juice (optional)	Salt the rim of a chilled margarita glass, if desired. Put ice cubes in a cocktail shaker. Add tequila, triple sec, and sour mix. Shake well. Pour the drink, along with the ice, into the chilled glass. Garnish with a lime wedge. Add a dash of lemon or lime juice.

May God grant you many years to live, for sure he must be knowing, the earth has angels all too few and heaven is overflowing. **Irish toast**

> **Tipsy Trivia**
> Remember your tequila etiquette: salt, lemon, *then* tequila shot. And, of course, say *gracias*.

Big Jug Wine Pasta

When the wine goes in, strange things come out.
—JOHANN CHRISTOPH FRIEDRICH VON SCHILLER

SERVES 3–4

3 quarts chicken stock

1 package linguine (12 ounces)

¼ cup extra virgin olive oil

½ teaspoon red pepper flakes

½ teaspoon oregano

2 cups red wine

4 cloves garlic, creamed with a pinch kosher salt

⅓ cup whipping cream

2 tablespoons fresh basil

½ cup pine nuts, toasted, for garnish

1. Place chicken stock in a large pot and bring to a boil. Follow the package directions to cook the pasta.
2. Place olive oil in a saucepan and heat over medium heat. Add red pepper flakes, oregano, and red wine. Bring to a boil. Reduce heat, keeping the sauce simmering until thickened. Add in the garlic. Finish the sauce by stirring in the whipping cream. Remove from heat.
3. Drain pasta and add to the sauce mixture. Toss with the fresh basil. Garnish with the toasted pine nuts and serve.

ALCOHOL CONTENT:

SUGGESTED PAIRING: Garlic bread

Drink Pairing: *Merlot*

May the doctor never earn a dollar out of you. **Various attributions**

> **Tipsy Trivia**
> Samuel Hanshall patented the corkscrew in England in 1795. Not to be outdone, François Rever patented the corkscrew in France in 1828. Finally, the United States caught up when M. L. Byrn patented the corkscrew in the United States in 1860.

Woozy Cod Swimming in Huckleberry Vodka

Always do sober what you said you'd do drunk. That will teach you to keep your mouth shut.

—ERNEST HEMINGWAY

SERVES 4

½ cup raspberry vinegar

¼ cup vegetable oil

½ shot huckleberry vodka

1 tablespoon sugar

1 tablespoon Dijon mustard

⅛ teaspoon salt

⅛ teaspoon pepper

4 cod fillets

1. To make the vinaigrette marinade, whisk together vinegar, oil, vodka, sugar, Dijon mustard, salt, and pepper.
2. Place cod fillets into a casserole dish and pour vinaigrette marinade over top. Allow to marinate for 20–30 minutes in the refrigerator.
3. Place fillets on aluminum foil. Grill over medium heat for approximately 3 minutes per side. Fish is done when it easily flakes with a fork.

ALCOHOL CONTENT:

SUGGESTED PAIRING: Sautéed broccoli with lemon juice and Parmesan cheese

Drink Pairing: *Sauvignon Blanc*

May the good Lord take a liking to you . . . but not too soon!
Traditional toast

> **Tipsy Trivia**
> Ohio law makes it illegal to get a fish drunk. So be sure to fillet the cod before you add the vodka.

Flying High Vodka Spinach Salad

I think a man ought to get drunk at least twice a year just on principle, so he won't let himself get snotty about it.

—**RAYMOND CHANDLER**

SERVES 2

⅓ cup red wine vinegar

½ cup sugar

2 tablespoons ginger vodka

1 teaspoon Dijon mustard

1 teaspoon salt

½ teaspoon pepper

2 tablespoons olive oil

1 tablespoon poppy seeds

4 cups spinach

1 hardboiled egg, sliced

3 cooked slices bacon, chopped

2 tablespoons sliced, toasted almonds

1. To make dressing, whisk together vinegar, sugar, vodka, Dijon mustard, salt, and pepper. Slowly whisk oil into dressing. Stir in poppy seeds.

2. In a large bowl, toss spinach with the dressing. Divide into two serving bowls. Top each bowl with half of the sliced hardboiled egg, chopped bacon, and almonds.

ALCOHOL CONTENT:

SUGGESTED PAIRING: Pita bread

Drink Pairing: *Ginger Spritz*	
1½ ounces ginger vodka 4 ounces sparkling wine, chilled	In a champagne flute, add ginger vodka, and chilled sparkling wine just prior to serving. Refreshing!

Do not walk in front of me, I may not follow. Do not walk behind me, I may not lead. Just walk beside me and be my friend. **Albert Camus**

Tipsy Trivia
Most fruits and vegetables contain sugar alcohol—yet another reason to love salad.

Raise Your Glass to Kindness!

Delusional Chicken in White Wine and Yogurt Sauce

A man who was fond of wine was offered some grapes at dessert after dinner. "Much obliged," said he, pushing the plate aside, "I am not accustomed to take my wine in pills."

—JEAN ANTHELME BRILLAT-SAVARIN

SERVES 4

4 boneless, skinless chicken breasts

3 tablespoons olive oil, divided

1 tablespoon butter

3 tablespoons all-purpose flour

½ cup chicken broth

½ cup low-fat yogurt

½ cup white wine

1 teaspoon black pepper

Salt to taste

½ cup sliced mushrooms

1. Preheat oven to 350°F. Place chicken in baking dish with butter and 2 tablespoons of the olive oil. Bake uncovered chicken for 20 minutes. Remove chicken from oven.

2. In a saucepan over medium heat, add remaining 1 tablespoon of oil. Stir in flour, chicken broth, yogurt, white wine, pepper, and salt to taste. Spread mushrooms evenly over chicken and pour sauce all over. Return dish to oven and cook for 30 more minutes or until chicken is tender.

ALCOHOL CONTENT:

SUGGESTED PAIRING: Steamed vegetable medley

Drink Pairing: *Chardonnay*

May your dog go out on time and your kids come home on time.
Author unknown

Tipsy Trivia

Vintners make white wine by removing the grape skins before fermentation. In a related fact, a study from the University of Florence suggests that women who drink two glasses of wine a day have better sex than nondrinkers.

Raise Your Glass to Imagination!

Shaken Gin Smoked Salmon Pasta

Once, during Prohibition, I was forced to live for days on nothing but food and water.
—**W. C. FIELDS**

SERVES 4

1 (16-ounce) package penne pasta

2 quarts chicken stock

2 tablespoons butter

1 tablespoon olive oil

½ onion, finely chopped

2 teaspoons garlic powder

½ cup milk

8 ounces Alfredo sauce

¼ cup dry gin or vodka

Salt and pepper to taste

10 ounces cooked smoked salmon, chopped

1 tablespoon fresh parsley, chopped

1. Bring pot of chicken stock to boil on stove. Add pasta and cook per directions on package. Drain and set aside.
2. Melt butter in a large skillet over medium heat. Add olive oil, and sauté onion until tender. Stir in garlic powder, milk, Alfredo sauce, and gin or vodka. Salt and pepper to taste. Heat to below boiling point until sauce is smooth, for 3–5 minutes.
3. Gently fold in salmon. Ladle over pasta. Garnish with parsley and serve.

ALCOHOL CONTENT:

SUGGESTED PAIRING: Mixed green salad

Drink pairing: *Chablis*

May the hinges of our friendship never grow rusty. **Traditional toast**

Tipsy Trivia
W. C. Fields drank two quarts of gin a day.

Raise Your Glass to Success!

Trippin' Whiskey Chicken Fettuccine Alfredo

I feel sorry for people who don't drink. When they wake up in the morning, that's as good as they're going to feel all day.

—FRANK SINATRA

SERVES 4

2 boneless, skinless chicken breasts

12 ounces fettuccine

Chicken stock as needed to prepare fettuccine

1 cup whipping cream

1 teaspoon basil

½ teaspoon garlic powder

1 ounce black cherry whiskey

1 egg yolk, beaten

Salt and pepper to taste

1½ cups finely grated Parmesan cheese

1 teaspoon parsley flakes, for garnish

1. Preheat grill to medium-high heat. Grill chicken breasts for approximately 4–6 minutes per side, until no longer pink and juices run clear.
2. Prepare fettuccine per package instructions, using chicken stock in place of water. Drain.
3. Heat cream in saucepan over medium heat. Slowly blend in cheese until melted. Continue to stir slowly while adding basil, garlic powder, and whiskey. Blend in egg yolk to thicken. Salt and pepper to taste. Allow to cool.
4. Cut cooked chicken breasts into bite-size pieces. Place chicken over fettuccine and spoon sauce over. Top with Parmesan cheese. Garnish with parsley flakes.

ALCOHOL CONTENT:

SUGGESTED PAIRING: Bread with Italian dipping oil

Drink pairing: *Sauvignon Blanc*

May we suffer as much sorrow as the drops of wine we are about to leave in our glasses! **Russian toast**

> **Tipsy Trivia**
> A closed bottle of whiskey can still be good to drink after 100 years. An open bottle of whiskey is good to drink today. Seems like no contest.

Sassy Salmon in Champagne Sauce

I envy people who drink—at least they know what to blame everything on.
—OSCAR LEVANT

SERVES 2

2 salmon fillets

1 tablespoon butter

1 tablespoon olive oil

1 teaspoon chopped shallots

½ cup champagne

½ cup heavy cream

½ cup sliced mushrooms, optional

Salt and pepper to taste

1 teaspoon tarragon, for garnish

1. Preheat grill to medium.
2. Lightly oil a sheet of aluminum foil and put that on top of the grill before placing the salmon on top. Grill the fish 4 minutes per side or until the fish is cooked through. Keep warm.
3. Add butter, olive oil, and shallots to a saucepan over medium heat. Cook for 1–2 minutes until the shallots turn translucent, then add the champagne to the pan and bring to a boil. Reduce to 2–3 tablespoons.
4. Add cream to reduced champagne mixture and bring to a boil. Stir occasionally to keep it from burning, until reduced by ½ or ⅓, depending on how saucy you like it! If desired, add mushrooms at the end of the reduction and reduce the heat to low for 2–3 minutes, until mushrooms are heated through.
5. Add salt and pepper to taste. Remove from heat.
6. Place fish on serving dish and drizzle champagne sauce over top. Sprinkle with tarragon and serve.

ALCOHOL CONTENT:

SUGGESTED PAIRING: Roasted potatoes with rosemary

Drink pairing: *Pinot Grigio*

May your pockets be heavy, your heart be light, and may good luck pursue you each morning and night. **Irish toast**

Tipsy Trivia

The French claim that the saucer-shaped champagne glass (shallow and wide-mouthed) was inspired by the breast of Marie Antoinette. The Greeks claim that the glass was inspired by the breast of Helen of Troy. Other claimants to the honor include Empress Josephine, Madame de Pompadour, and the mistress of Henry II.

Raise Your Glass to Spontaneity!

Submerged Vodka Veggie Sub

Even though a number of people have tried, no one has yet found a way to drink for a living.

—**JEAN KERR**

SERVES 1

2 tablespoons mayonnaise

½ shot cucumber vodka

1 sub roll, sliced in half lengthwise

⅓ cup fresh spinach

2 teaspoons black olives

4 tomato slices

3 onion slices

4 cucumber slices

3 tablespoons mushrooms, sliced

Alfalfa sprouts, to taste

1–2 cheese slices, your choice

Salt and pepper

1. Mix mayonnaise and cucumber vodka in bowl. Spread mayonnaise mix on both sides of a sub roll.
2. On bottom roll of sub add spinach, black olives, tomato, onion, cucumbers, mushrooms, alfalfa sprouts, and cheese. Sprinkle salt and pepper to taste. Place top of sub roll onto sandwich and enjoy!

ALCOHOL CONTENT:

SUGGESTED PAIRING: Fruit salad

Drink pairing: *Zinfandel*

To catching up! May we visit more often! **Russian toast**

> **Tipsy Trivia**
> Russians liked the fact that you could transport vodka through frigid temperatures and it still wouldn't freeze. We recommend testing this by keeping a bottle of Grey Goose in your freezer.

Another Round White Wine Linguine Shrimp

It takes only one drink to get me drunk. The trouble is, I can't remember if it's the thirteenth or the fourteenth.

—GEORGE BURNS

SERVES 2

½ pound linguine

Chicken stock to prepare linguine

1 tablespoon olive oil

½ tablespoon garlic powder

¼ teaspoon crushed red pepper flakes

2 tablespoons butter

½ pound shrimp, peeled and deveined
 with tails removed

¾ cup white wine

1 teaspoon lemon tea vodka

Salt and pepper to taste

½ teaspoon, or to taste, fresh parsley,
 finely chopped (optional)

1. Cook the linguine per package directions, using chicken stock instead of water. Drain and set aside.
2. Heat olive oil in a large skillet over medium heat. Add garlic powder and red pepper flakes and cook for 1–2 minutes. Reduce heat to medium-low.
3. Melt in the butter, then add the shrimp. Add white wine and bring to a boil.
4. Lower heat and simmer for another 3–4 minutes until the white wine has reduced by ⅓. Add lemon tea vodka. Add salt and pepper to taste.
5. Place cooked linguine in a large bowl. Pour wine sauce over the linguine. Mix pasta and sauce together to cover all the linguine. If desired, add parsley to garnish and serve.

ALCOHOL CONTENT:

SUGGESTED PAIRING: Spinach salad

Drink pairing: *Zinfandel*

May God bless and keep the Tsar . . . far away from us. **Rabbi in** *Fiddler on the Roof*

> **Tipsy Trivia**
> The red substance at the bottom of a wine glass is tannin. It is an excellent antioxidant and another good reason to drain your glass.

Raise Your Glass to Opportunity!

Keg o' Beer Hot Dogs

Oh, you hate your job? Why didn't you say so? There's a support group for that. It's called everybody. They meet at the bar.

—DREW CAREY

SERVES 8

2 bottles of beer, light or dark
1 package of 8 hot dogs
8 hot dog buns
Ketchup (optional)
Mustard (optional)
Relish (optional)

1. Place a large pot on the stove on medium heat. Pour in the beer until close to ¾ full but do not overfill. You want to leave enough room for 8 hot dogs to boil without overflowing. Once the beer is boiling, gently place the hot dogs into the pot. Follow the directions on the hot dog package to get the desired doneness.
2. Once the hot dogs are cooked, place hot dogs on buns and add desired condiments (ketchup, mustard, and relish) on top. Enjoy!

ALCOHOL CONTENT (AS LONG AS YOU DON'T DRINK THE BOILED BEER!):

SUGGESTED PAIRING: Baked beans

Drink pairing: *Pilsner*

May you have all the happiness and luck that life can hold and at the end of all your rainbows may you find a pot of gold. **Irish toast**

Raise Your Glass to Great Food!

Peanut Butter and Vodka Jelly Sandwich

The first time I played the Masters, I was so nervous I drank a bottle of rum before I teed off. I shot the happiest 83 of my life.

—**CHI CHI RODRIGUEZ**

SERVES 2

4 tablespoons raspberry or grape jelly

1 teaspoon raspberry or grape vodka

4 slices white bread

4 tablespoons peanut butter

1. Mix jelly with vodka in a bowl. Spread peanut butter on 2 slices of bread and jelly mixture on the other two. Makes 2 sandwiches.

ALCOHOL CONTENT:

SUGGESTED PAIRING: Potato chips

Drink pairing: *Never Mind the Name*	
1–2 cups ice 1½ ounces Chambord 2 ounces Irish cream 4 ounces milk	Fill a cocktail shaker with ice. Pour all other ingredients over ice and shake well. Strain into a chilled 8-ounce glass.

May you never have bitter moments, hear salty jokes, or see sour smiles. Let's drink to the sweet sides of life! **Russian toast**

Tipsy Trivia
It is illegal to describe any alcoholic beverage as "refreshing." "Inebriating" is still okay.

Raise Your Glass to Possibilities!

Ham and Cheesy Champagne Sandwich

There's nothing wrong with sobriety in moderation.

> —**JOHN CANDY**

SERVES 1

1 tablespoon champagne

¼ cup poppy seed dressing

2 pieces of your favorite bread

3 slices ham

2 slices Swiss cheese

Lettuce and tomato (optional)

1. In a small bowl, combine champagne and poppy seed dressing.
2. Spread champagne/poppy seed dressing onto both sides of bread. Place cheese and ham on bread. If desired, add lettuce or tomato. Enjoy!

ALCOHOL CONTENT:

SUGGESTED PAIRING: Sweet potato wedges

Drink pairing: *Belgian White Ale*

Let others praise ancient times; I am glad I was born in these.
Ovid (43 B.C.–18 A.D.)

Tipsy Trivia

Champagne is sparkling wine from the Champagne region of France. Sparkling wine from any place else must be called . . . "sparkling wine."

Raise Your Glass to Peace!

Punchy Rum Runner Chicken

I always wake up at the crack of ice.
—JOE E. LEWIS

SERVES 4

1 tablespoon extra-virgin olive oil

1 garlic clove, chopped

1 cup onions, chopped

2 tablespoons lime juice

¼ cup rum

4 tablespoons brown sugar

4 boneless, skinless chicken breasts

1 lime, cut into wedges

1. Heat a pan with olive oil over medium heat. Add garlic and onions. Sauté until garlic is lightly browned and the onions are soft and clear.
2. In a bowl, combine lime juice, rum, and brown sugar, with sautéed garlic and onions to make marinade.
3. Place chicken breasts into a resealable plastic bag and pour in marinade. Refrigerate overnight or for 2–3 hours.
4. Preheat the oven to 350°F. Place chicken with marinade in baking dish. Bake the uncovered chicken for 45 minutes or until juices run clear.
5. Remove chicken from baking dish. Squeeze lime wedges over chicken and serve.

ALCOHOL CONTENT:

SUGGESTED PAIRING: Steamed squash

Drink pairing: *A Tropical Dream*	
1 ounce coconut rum 1 ounce Blue Curaçao liqueur 1 ounce pineapple juice 1 cherry or lime (optional)	In a shaker, mix the rum, Curaçao, and pineapple juice. Pour into a cocktail glass. Garnish with a cherry or lime on the glass rim.

Blessed are the rum drinkers, for they get to drink rum. **Author unknown**

> **Tipsy Trivia**
> Rum was the world's first distilled spirit and, of course, the favorite of Caribbean pirates.

Raise Your Glass to Romance!

Mellow Tilapia with White Wine and Lemon Sauce

My grandmother is over eighty and still doesn't need glasses. Drinks right out of the bottle.
—**HENNY YOUNGMAN**

SERVES 2

2 tablespoons olive oil, divided

2 tilapia fillets

1 onion, chopped

½ cup white wine

2 tablespoons butter

1 tablespoon fresh parsley

1 teaspoon lemon vodka

Salt to taste

1. Preheat the grill to medium.
2. Oil 2 pieces of aluminum foil with 1 tablespoon olive oil. Wrap fish in the foil and cook away from direct heat, about 10 minutes until fish is cooked thoroughly.
3. While fish is cooking, prepare sauce. Heat remaining 1 tablespoon olive oil in a pan over medium heat. Add onions and cook until softened, around 1 minute.
4. Add in wine and bring to a boil until wine reduces to around ¼ of a cup. This can take a little less than 5 minutes. Remove from heat source. Add the butter, parsley, lemon vodka, and salt.
5. Place fish on a platter and drizzle the sauce on top of the fish.

ALCOHOL CONTENT:

SUGGESTED PAIRING: Cherry tomatoes

Drink pairing: *Chardonnay*

From wine what sudden friendship springs! **John Gay**

> **Tipsy Trivia**
> A red grape can make white wine, but a white grape cannot make red wine.

Champagne Oysters Rockefeller

I have taken more out of alcohol than alcohol has taken out of me.
—**WINSTON CHURCHILL**

SERVES 6–12

¼ cup champagne

2 cups spinach, finely chopped

2 green onions, finely chopped

½ cup coarse bread crumbs, divided

1 tablespoon fresh parsley, finely chopped

3 tablespoons butter

Salt and pepper, to taste

24 fresh oysters on half shell

¼ cup fresh grated Parmesan cheese

10 cups kosher salt

Lemon wedges and/or parsley for garnish

1. Preheat barbecue grill to medium.
2. In a bowl combine champagne, spinach, onions, ¼ cup of the bread crumbs, and parsley.
3. In a skillet, melt butter over medium heat. Add champagne–bread-crumb mixture. Cook 1–2 minutes, stirring until spinach is wilted.
4. Sprinkle with salt and pepper to taste. Remove from heat.
5. Place oysters in the shell on a baking sheet. Put 1 tablespoon of champagne–bread-crumb mixture on each oyster. Sprinkle remaining bread crumbs and Parmesan cheese on top of oysters.
6. Place baking sheet on the barbecue grill. Grill for about 5 minutes, with the lid closed, or until cheese is bubbling and is starting to brown.
7. Cover the bottom of a shallow serving platter with a layer of kosher salt.
8. Remove oysters from baking sheet. Place oysters on the salted shallow serving platter. Garnish with lemon wedges and/or parsley.

ALCOHOL CONTENT:

Drink pairing: *Rosé*

Candy is dandy, but liquor is quicker. **Ogden Nash**

> **Tipsy Trivia**
> **A champagne cork can leave the bottle at 100 mph. Duck!**

Tanked Tequila Fish Tacos

I'm not quite sure where I stand on the legalization of drugs—though, if tequila is legal, pot should probably be legal.

—TED DEMME

SERVES 4

¼ tablespoon olive oil

Juice from 1 lime

½ shot tequila

¼ cup fresh cilantro leaves, chopped

2 cod or tilapia fillets (can also use mahi mahi)

Salt and pepper to taste

8 corn tortillas, warmed

Sour cream, for garnish

Capers, for garnish

Avocado, for garnish

Premade salsa of your choice, for garnish

1. Preheat grill to medium heat.
2. Mix olive oil, lime juice, tequila, and cilantro in a shallow bowl. Add the fish to the bowl. Marinate for 20 minutes.
3. Lightly oil on the grill to help keep the fish from sticking during grilling. Place fish on the grill and let cook for around 4 minutes over direct heat. Be careful not to burn. Flip the fish and let grill for 1 minute. Make sure the fish is cooked thoroughly. Let the fish rest for about 5 minutes. Flake the fish into pieces.
4. Place fish pieces in corn tortillas. Add garnishes to taste.

ALCOHOL CONTENT:

SUGGESTED PAIRING: Corn salad

Drink pairing: *Belgian white ale*

Oh to be seventy again! **Oliver Wendell Holmes Jr., at age eighty-five**

> **Tipsy Trivia**
> **There is actually a town called Tequila, Mexico—birthplace of tequila.** *Vamanos!*

Beer Barrel Chili

Without question, the greatest invention in the history of mankind is beer. Oh, I grant you that the wheel was also a fine invention, but the wheel does not go nearly as well with pizza.

—DAVE BARRY

SERVES 8–10

1½ pounds ground beef

1 12-ounce beer

1 large yellow onion, chopped

1 clove garlic, minced

½ jalapeño, seeded and minced

1 8-ounce can red kidney beans

1 8-ounce can chili beans

1 8-ounce can Rotel diced tomatoes

3 tablespoons chili powder

1 teaspoon cumin

½ teaspoon cayenne pepper

½ teaspoon salt

½ teaspoon pepper

1. In a skillet on medium heat, brown ground beef. Drain and place into saucepan on medium heat.
2. Add remaining ingredients and stir, bringing pot to a boil. Reduce heat to a simmer. Partially cover pot and allow to cook for 1½ hours. Serve.

ALCOHOL CONTENT:

SUGGESTED PAIRING: Cornbread

Drink pairing: *Dark lager*

May your car start and your hangover stop. **Author unknown**

> **Tipsy Trivia**
> **Beer is the most popular alcoholic beverage in the world. Only water and tea beat beer in worldwide popularity.**

Raise Your Glass to New Beginnings!

Beer, Meet Vodka Marinated Chicken Wings

Health—what my friends are always drinking to before they fall down.

—PHYLLIS DILLER

SERVES 2

10 chicken wings

Marinade

¼ cup olive oil

2 teaspoons ginger vodka

½ cup light beer or lager

¼ cup light soy sauce

2 tablespoons lemon juice

½ teaspoon salt

¼ teaspoon pepper

¼ teaspoon paprika

2 teaspoons garlic powder

Cream Sauce

Reserved marinade

1 tablespoon brown sugar

Couple splashes Tabasco sauce (to desired spiciness level)

¼ cup whipping cream

1 tablespoon butter

1. Place chicken wings in a resealable plastic bag.
2. In a small bowl, mix together all marinade ingredients. Add marinade to the bag and coat chicken wings. Put plastic bag in a bowl so the mixture does not leak, and marinate in the refrigerator for 24 hours.
3. Preheat oven to 350°F.
4. Place chicken wings in a baking dish, reserving the marinade to use to make a sauce. Bake chicken at 350°F for about 1 hour until wings are cooked through.
5. While the chicken cooks, make the sauce. In a saucepan pour in the remaining marinade and heat over medium heat until bubbly and thickened. Whisk in brown sugar, Tabasco, and cream. Return to heat until bubbling. To finish, whisk in butter until melted. Turn off the heat and pour sauce over the cooked wings. Enjoy!

ALCOHOL CONTENT:

Drink pairing: *Same beer used in cooking.*

For the vodka, a glass, for the beer, a mug, and for the table, cheerful company. **Russian toast**

> ### Tipsy Trivia
> [. . .] our victuals [were] much spent, especially our beer," wrote colonists William Bradford and Edward Winslow, explaining why the *Mayflower* would divert to Plymouth. Those Pilgrims had their priorities straight."

Infused White Wine Shrimp Alfredo

My dad was the town drunk. Usually that's not so bad, but New York City?
—**HENNY YOUNGMAN**

SERVES 3–4

12 ounces linguine

2 quarts chicken stock

1 cup whipping cream

1½ cups finely grated Parmesan

1 teaspoon basil

½ teaspoon garlic powder

1 teaspoon parsley flakes

Salt and pepper, to taste

2 tablespoons white wine

1 egg yolk, beaten

2 tablespoons extra-virgin olive oil

1 pound shrimp, peeled and deveined

1. Boil linguine in chicken stock per package instructions. Drain and set aside.
2. Heat cream in saucepan over medium heat. Slowly blend in cheese until melted. Continue to stir slowly while adding spices and white wine.
3. Blend in egg yolk to thicken; keep warm.
4. Heat a pan with oil on medium heat and add shrimp. Cook for approximately 5 minutes or until meat turns opaque and skin turns pink. Place shrimp over linguine and spoon sauce over top. Serve.

ALCOHOL CONTENT:

SUGGESTED PAIRING: Bread sticks

Drink pairing: *Pinot Grigio*

Let us have wine and women, mirth and laughter, sermons and soda water the day after. **Lord Byron**

> **Tipsy Trivia**
> **Toasting Etiquette: If you are the subject of a toast (the toastee, as it were) then you do not stand or drink. You simply smile and say "Thank you" when the toast is over.**

Raise Your Glass to Fun!

Bar Tab Vodka Pasta Salad

Are you there vodka? It's me, Chelsea. Please get me out of jail and I promise I will never drink again.

—CHELSEA HANDLER

SERVES 6

8 ounces rotini pasta

2 quarts chicken or vegetable stock

1 cup Italian salad dressing

1 tablespoon vodka

2 tomatoes, chopped

1 cucumber, sliced

⅓ cup pitted black olives, sliced

Salt and pepper to taste

1. Cook pasta in chicken or vegetable stock according to package directions. Drain and chill.
2. In a small bowl mix Italian dressing and vodka.
3. In a large bowl, combine pasta, tomatoes, cucumber, olives, and salt and pepper. Toss well with dressing. Serve chilled or at room temperature.

ALCOHOL CONTENT:

SUGGESTED PAIRING: Pita bread

Drink pairing: *Chianti*

May all your troubles during the coming year be as short-lived as your New Year's resolutions. **Brian Vaszily**

Thousand Island Vodka Hamburgers

You're only as young as the women you feel.
—GROUCHO MARX

SERVES 4

½ cup Thousand Island dressing

1 teaspoon vodka

1¼ pounds ground beef

½ teaspoon salt

½ teaspoon freshly ground black pepper

4 hamburger buns

Tomatoes, sliced

Lettuce leaves

1. Preheat grill on high heat.
2. In a bowl, combine Thousand Island dressing and vodka.
3. Mix ground beef, salt, and pepper using your hands. Form 4 patties.
4. Place patties on grill. Cook burgers for 5 minutes per side, or until well done. Place cooked hamburgers on buns. Top with Thousand Island dressing mixture, tomatoes, and lettuce and serve.

ALCOHOL CONTENT:

SUGGESTED PAIRING: French fries

Drink pairing: *Beaujolais*

Here's to gaining wealth and losing weight. **Author unknown**

> **Tipsy Trivia**
> Magellan spent more money on sherry than weapons when stocking his ships to sail around the world. There is a lesson there for all of us.

Raise Your Glass to Curiosity!

Yo Ho Ho Rum Pork Chop Sandwich

Sometimes too much to drink is barely enough.

—MARK TWAIN

SERVES 2

1 teaspoon rum

1 tablespoon soy sauce

½ teaspoon chili powder

¼ teaspoon oregano

¼ teaspoon thyme

¼ teaspoon salt

¼ teaspoon pepper

2 boneless pork chops

4 slices favorite cheese (optional)

2 hamburger buns

Lettuce leaves for garnish

2 slices tomato

1. Preheat grill on medium-high.
2. Mix rum, soy sauce, chili powder, oregano, thyme, salt, and pepper together. Rub half of marinade on the pork chops.
3. Place pork chops on the grill. They can dry out quickly so keep a close watch. The average cooking time for 1-inch thick pork chops is 5–7 minutes per side. If desired, add cheese and cook until just melted. Remove pork chops from grill when cooked through.
4. Quickly put the remaining half of the marinade on top of the pork chops for about 2 minutes before serving to add extra flavor.
5. Serve on bun with lettuce and tomato.

ALCOHOL CONTENT:

SUGGESTED PAIRING: Coleslaw

Drink pairing: *Sea Breeze*	
1–2 cups ice 1½ ounces vodka 4 ounces grapefruit juice 1½ ounces cranberry juice 1 lime wedge	Fill a highball glass with ice. Pour vodka, grapefruit juice, and cranberry juice over the ice. Garnish with a lime wedge.

Love, health, money, and time to enjoy it. **Frank Basile**

> **Tipsy Trivia**
> Canada has a 300-year-old tradition of trading dried cod fish for rum. Those crafty Canadians are definitely getting the better end of that bargain.

Raise Your Glass to Surprises!

Tropical Cruise Ginger Vodka Asian Salad

I saw a notice that said "Drink Canada Dry" and I've just started.

—BRENDAN BEHAN

SERVES 2–3

1 pound sirloin steak

Marinade

3 garlic cloves, minced

4 green onions, chopped

3 tablespoons low-calorie soy sauce

2 tablespoons olive oil

2 tablespoons rice wine vinegar

2 tablespoons sesame oil

¼ teaspoon curry powder

2 tablespoons ginger vodka

1 tablespoon brown sugar

Salad

6 cups mixed salad greens

1 red bell pepper, chopped

1 8-ounce can water chestnuts, drained
and chopped

1. Place steak in a plastic bag.
2. Combine all marinade ingredients in a bowl. Mix well and pour ½ into the bag with steak. Let marinate for 2–3 hours in the refrigerator. Save rest of unused marinade for dressing the salad.
3. Preheat grill. Grill steak until cooked for desired doneness. Cut into ⅛" strips.
4. Mix cooked steak with salad greens, chopped bell pepper, and water chestnuts. Pour remaining marinade over salad. Serve.

ALCOHOL CONTENT:

SUGGESTED PAIRING: Noodles

Drink pairing: *Sake, warmed*

May you always work like you don't need the money. May you always love like you've never been hurt. May you always dance like there's nobody watching. **Various attributions**

> **Tipsy Trivia**
> **Okhotnichya, also known as Hunter's Vodka, is flavored with herbs and spices including ginger, anise, and cloves—just the thing for chasing wolves across the Russian countryside.**

Captain's Table Bourbon Pulled-Pork Sandwich

A man can take a little bourbon without getting drunk, but if you hold his mouth open and pour in a quart, he's going to get sick on it.

—LYNDON B. JOHNSON

SERVES 1

1 serving packaged pulled pork

¼ to ½ cup favorite barbecue sauce, depending on how saucy you want the barbecue

1 tablespoon bourbon

1 hamburger bun

1. Cook or reheat the pulled pork following the directions on the package.
2. Simmer barbecue sauce and bourbon in a pan for 2–3 minutes. Do not burn. Turn off pan and add the warmed pulled pork to the barbecue sauce. Stir and mix pulled pork and barbecue together.
3. Place pulled pork on the hamburger bun and serve.

ALCOHOL CONTENT:

SUGGESTED PAIRING: Coleslaw

Drink pairing: *Mint Julep*	
2–3 fresh mint leaves 1 teaspoon sugar 1–2 cups ice 1½ ounces bourbon whiskey 1 mint sprig, for garnish	Muddle mint leaves and sugar in a Collins glass. Fill with ice and whiskey. Stir. Decorate with mint sprig.

Live each day as if it is your last, and each night as if it was your first.
Shep Hyken

Tipsy Trivia
Bourbon is whiskey made in the United States in the same way that Scotch is whiskey made in Scotland. There is no official word for whiskey made in your cellar.

Windex Greek Gin Salad

A good heavy book holds you down. It's the anchor that keeps you from getting up and having another gin and tonic.

—ROY BLOUNT JR.

SERVES 3–4

2 Roma tomatoes, chopped

½ cucumber, seeded and chopped

3 ounces pitted kalamata olives

3 ounces feta cheese, crumbled

½ red onion, thinly sliced

12 romaine lettuce leaves

3 tablespoons pumpkin seeds, toasted

2 tablespoons olive oil

1 teaspoon garlic powder

½ teaspoon oregano

3 tablespoons fresh basil, snipped

2 limes, juiced

2 teaspoons gin

1½ tablespoons sugar

¼ teaspoon salt

1. Mix tomato, cucumber, olives, feta cheese, red onion, romaine lettuce, and pumpkin seeds in a large serving bowl.
2. In a separate bowl, whisk olive oil, garlic powder, oregano, basil, lime juice, gin, sugar, and salt. Toss with salad ingredients. Serve.

ALCOHOL CONTENT:

SUGGESTED PAIRING: Bruschetta

Drink pairing: *Dirty Martini*	
1–2 cups ice 3 ounces vodka 1 ounce dry vermouth 1 ounce brine from olive jar 2 stuffed green olives, for garnish	Fill a cocktail shaker with ice. Pour all liquids over the ice. Shake well. Strain drink into a chilled cocktail glass. Garnish with an olive or two.

Enjoy life until your last breath. There is no drinking after death.
Author unknown

Tipsy Trivia
Prohibition was a great boon to gin production in the United States, encouraging the invention of bathtub gin.

Mix Drinks Like a Pro Whiskey Steak and Cheese Sandwich

My favorite animal is steak.
—**FRAN LEBOWITZ**

SERVES 4

3 tablespoons olive oil, divided

1 onion, cut in thin slices

1 tablespoon whiskey

1 pound beef sirloin, sliced very thin

4 slices Provolone cheese

4 hoagie rolls

1. In a skillet, add 1 tablespoon olive oil over medium heat. Place onions in pan and cook until translucent, 2–3 minutes. Remove onions and set aside.
2. Turn down heat so oil does not splatter and add remaining 2 tablespoons of olive oil and whiskey to skillet. Sauté the slices of meat quickly on both sides.
3. Put cheese and onions on top of meat just before meat has finished cooking and cover skillet until cheese melts.
4. Place equal amounts of meat-cheese-and-onion mixture in each roll. Serve.

ALCOHOL CONTENT:

SUGGESTED PAIRING: French fries

Drink pairing: *Bourbon Old Fashioned*	
3 dashes bitters 1 sugar cube or 1 teaspoon sugar 1 teaspoon water 1–2 cups ice 3 ounces bourbon whiskey 1 slice orange, for garnish 1 maraschino cherry, for garnish	Mix bitters, sugar cube, and water in an old-fashioned glass. Fill glass almost full with ice cubes and add the bourbon. Garnish with an orange slice and a maraschino cherry.

Here's to you, here's to me . . . may we never disagree. But if we do, the hell with you . . . here's to me! **John Patrick Dolan**

> ### Tipsy Trivia
> Whiskey made from rye is stronger than whiskey made from corn. This is because the rye grain is smaller than the corn grain. We always knew that size mattered.

Veni Vidi Vici Vodka Caesar Salad

Money, like vodka, turns a person into an eccentric.
—ANTON CHEKHOV

SERVES 4–6

1 head romaine lettuce, chopped or torn into small pieces

½ to 1 cup Caesar dressing, to taste

1 tablespoon vodka

1 bag Caesar salad croutons

6 tablespoons grated Parmesan cheese

1. Place chopped or torn lettuce in a bowl.
2. In another bowl, add Caesar salad dressing and vodka. Mix well.
3. Drizzle dressing over lettuce and gently mix. Add croutons and Parmesan cheese on top. Serve.

ALCOHOL CONTENT:

SUGGESTED PAIRING: Garlic bread

Drink pairing: *Vodka Gimlet*	
1–2 cups ice 1 ounce lime juice 1 tablespoon simple syrup 2 ounces vodka	Fill a cocktail shaker with ice. Pour lime juice, syrup, and vodka over the ice. Strain into a cocktail glass.

Pay no attention to what critics say. There has never been a statue set up in honor of a critic. **Joyce Gibb**

Tipsy Trivia
If you know how to make a martini then you know how to make a Gibson. Just throw two or three cocktail olives into your martini and voilà! You have a Gibson.

Raise Your Glass to Grace!

Distracted Mussels in White Wine Sauce

There are two kinds of people I don't trust: people who don't drink and people who collect stickers.
—**CHELSEA HANDLER**

SERVES 2

2 tablespoons butter

2 tablespoons olive oil

¼ cup shallots, chopped

2 cloves garlic, minced

1 cup white wine

1–2 tablespoons parsley, chopped

1 pound mussels

Salt and pepper

1. Melt butter and olive oil over medium-low heat in a large pot. Toss in shallots and garlic and cook until translucent.
2. Add white wine, parsley, and mussels. Bring to a boil. Stir the pot, then cover for 8–10 minutes.
3. Remove pot from heat and dispose of unopened mussels. Season with salt and pepper. Serve.

ALCOHOL CONTENT:

SUGGESTED PAIRING: Artisan bread

Drink pairing: *Moselle wine*

To the old guard, the older we grow, the more we take and the less we know. At least the young men tell us so, but the day will come, when they shall know exactly how far a glass can go. To win the battle, 'gainst age, the foe. Here's youth . . . in a glass of wine. **James Monroe McLean**

> **Tipsy Trivia**
> Wine and grape juice have about the same number of calories. Use your calories wisely.

Raise Your Glass to Children Moving Out!

Quarters Bourbon BBQ Meatballs

The trouble with jogging is that the ice falls out of your glass.
—**MARTIN MULL**

SERVES 4–6

1 1-pound package premade meatballs
½ cup plain barbecue sauce
1 tablespoon bourbon

1. Cook the meatballs according to package directions. Put in a serving bowl.
2. Warm the barbecue sauce in a small saucepan. Add bourbon. Mix together and simmer for 1 minute.
3. Pour the warm barbecue sauce into another serving bowl. People can take a meatball and dip it in the barbecue sauce. No double dipping allowed, until everyone is sauced!

ALCOHOL CONTENT:

SUGGESTED PAIRING: Corn on the cob

Drink pairing: *Doctor's Orders*	
1½ ounces bourbon 4 ounces Dr. Pepper soda	Fill an old-fashioned glass with ice. Add bourbon and Dr. Pepper.

Go Wildcats! **University of Kentucky cheer**

> **Tipsy Trivia**
> U.S. law requires that all whiskeys be no less than 80 proof. USA! USA!

Raise Your Glass to Moving Out of Your Parents' House!

CHAPTER 3

Dinner

There's no better way of kicking back after a hard day than to have a nice dinner with a bottle of wine and then opening a bottle of something else. Whether you're eating alone or with friends, the pleasant feeling of a full stomach and an empty bottle gives you the reprieve you need to start the next day with a positive attitude.

Dinner is not only good for unwinding, it's the best way to catch up with friends, exchanging stories about rough patches and new successes. The easy laughter and good times that come with a hot meal and a cold drink bring us closer to those we cherish.

In this chapter we'll make dinners for all occasions from fancy red snapper, to flaming fajitas, to tasty steaks. We'll make salmon and shrimp, beer bites, and beef stew, and lamb chops to pork chops—dinner for all occasions.

Remember the toasts, raise your glasses, and *bon appétit*.

Slap-Happy Flaming Rum Fajitas

Why is the rum gone?
—**CAPTAIN JACK SPARROW**

SERVES 6

Juice of 1 lime

3 large cloves garlic, minced

½ tablespoon ground black pepper

¼ cup rum

1½ pounds very lean skirt steak, cut into ¼" thick strips

2 tablespoons olive oil, divided

1 large onion, cut into strips

1 yellow pepper, cut into strips

1 red pepper, cut into strips

1 green pepper, cut into strips

6 12" flour tortillas, warmed/blistered

Salsa, to taste (optional)

Chopped fresh cilantro, to taste (optional)

Sour cream, to taste (optional)

Guacamole, to taste (optional)

1. Place sliced steak into a resealable plastic bag.
2. Combine lime juice, garlic, ground pepper, and rum in a bowl, then add to the plastic bag and coat the steak thoroughly. Marinate in the refrigerator for several hours.
3. Add 1 tablespoon of olive oil to a skillet and heat over medium heat. Sear meat on both sides. Set meat aside.
4. Add remaining olive oil and onion to pan. Cook over medium heat until onion is soft and translucent. Return steak to the pan. Add bell peppers. When the peppers are tender, remove pan from heat.
5. Serve fajitas with tortillas. Garnish with salsa, cilantro, sour cream, and guacamole, if desired.

ALCOHOL CONTENT:

SUGGESTED PAIRING: Spanish rice and refried beans

Drink Pairing: *Margarita Martini*	
1–2 cups ice 5 ounces tequila 1 ounce Cointreau 1 ounce Grand Marnier 2 ounces freshly squeezed lime juice 1 ounce simple syrup Salt (optional) 1 lime wedge	Fill a cocktail shaker with ice. Add all ingredients. Shake well. Strain into a chilled martini glass. Garnish with salt and lime wedge.

This here's the wattle, the emblem of our land. You can stick it in a bottle, you can hold it in your hand. Amen! **Eric Idle as Bruce from** *Monty Python* **TV Series**

Happy Hour Clam Beer Bites

The best beer in the world is the open bottle in your hand!
—**DANNY JANSEN**

MAKES 36 PIECES

1 stick butter, room temperature

½ cup fine bread crumbs

¼ cup beer

1 cup onion, minced

2 cloves garlic, minced

2 tablespoons chopped fresh parsley

1 teaspoon basil

½ teaspoon oregano

½ teaspoon rosemary

⅛ teaspoon ground red pepper

Salt and pepper, to taste

4 small cans minced clams (6½ ounces each), drained (reserve the juice)

36 baguette slices, toasted

½ cup grated Parmesan cheese

1. Preheat oven to 375°F.
2. In a large bowl, combine all ingredients except the clams, baguette slices, and Parmesan cheese.
3. Mix clams into bread crumb mixture. If mixture is too dry, add additional clam juice. Spread mixture on the toasted baguette slices.
4. Bake for 8–10 minutes. Remove from oven and put Parmesan cheese on top. Turn the oven to broil. Put the baguette slices back in the oven and broil until golden.

ALCOHOL CONTENT:

Drink Pairing: *Hefeweizen*

Come, my lad, and drink some beer. **Samuel Johnson**

Half-Seas over Lime Rum Shrimp Kebabs

When I read about the evils of drinking, I gave up reading.
—**HENNY YOUNGMAN**

SERVES 8

2 shots lime rum, divided

½ cup chicken or shrimp stock

2 pounds jumbo shrimp, peeled and deveined

¼ teaspoon salt

¼ teaspoon black pepper

Juice of 1 lime

2 large onions, cut into 8 wedges

16 large mushrooms

2 large green peppers, cut into 1½" pieces

16 cherry tomatoes

1. In a large resealable plastic bag, combine 1 shot lime rum, stock, shrimp, salt, and pepper. Seal bag and turn to coat shrimp. Refrigerate for 30 minutes, turning occasionally. Drain and discard marinade.
2. In a clean bowl, make a lime sauce by mixing 1 shot of lime rum and fresh lime juice and set aside.
3. Alternate shrimp and vegetables on each of 8 skewers. You can use metal skewers or wood ones (soak in water first). Baste quickly with lime sauce. Over medium heat with the lid closed, grill kebabs for 3 minutes on each side or until shrimp are cooked. Baste with lime sauce before serving.

ALCOHOL CONTENT:

SUGGESTED PAIRING: Rice pilaf

Drink Pairing: *Mojito*	
4 mint leaves	1. In a Collins glass, combine mint leaves and sugar. Add the lime juice over them and mix together.
1 tablespoon sugar	
Juice of 1 lime	2. Add crushed ice to the glass. Mix in the rum. Pour in the club soda. Add sprig of mint for garnish.
2 ounces white rum	
2 ounces club soda	
1 sprig mint (for garnish)	

Tipsy Trivia
James Bond liked his martinis shaken, not stirred—unless he was in Cuba (in *Die Another Day*); then he ordered a mojito.

May your heart be light and happy, may your smile be big and wide, and may your pockets always have a coin or two inside! **Traditional toast**

Raise Your Glass to Forgiveness!

Honey I'm Home Whiskey Chicken

If you drink, don't drive. Don't even putt.
—DEAN MARTIN

SERVES 4

4 skinless, boneless chicken breasts

2 tablespoons olive oil

1 green onion, diced

¼ cup soy sauce

2 tablespoons red wine vinegar

2 tablespoons honey whiskey

2 tablespoons brown sugar

1 tablespoon diced fresh ginger

2 cloves garlic, minced

¼ teaspoon salt

¼ teaspoon freshly ground black pepper

1. Set chicken breasts in a small baking dish.
2. In a separate bowl, mix oil, onion, soy sauce, vinegar, whiskey, sugar, ginger, garlic, salt, and pepper. Pour over the chicken. Marinate in the refrigerator overnight or for at least 1 hour.
3. Preheat the oven to 350°F. Bake the uncovered chicken in the marinade for 45 minutes or until juices run clear. Baste several times during cooking. Serve.

ALCOHOL CONTENT:

SUGGESTED PAIRING: Twice-baked potatoes

Drink Pairing: *Whiskey Sour*	
2 ounces whiskey 1 ounce sweet-and-sour mix	Fill an old-fashioned glass with ice. Pour whiskey and sweet-and-sour mix over the ice cubes and mix.

Always remember to forget the troubles that passed away. But never forget to remember the blessings that come each day. **Traditional toast**

> **Tipsy Trivia**
> Mead is made from honey and was one of the world's first fermented beverages. Some say that we get the word "honeymoon" from the European tradition of supplying a newly married couple with a month's worth of mead.

Raise Your Glass to Strength!

Bloody Mary Vodka Spaghetti

I have to think hard to name an interesting man who does not drink.

—RICHARD BURTON

SERVES 4

2 quarts chicken stock

12 ounces spaghetti

2 tablespoons olive oil

1 medium onion, chopped

1 medium red bell pepper, chopped

4 cloves garlic, chopped

1 6-ounce can tomato paste

2 14.5-ounce cans diced tomatoes

1 teaspoon basil

2 teaspoons oregano

1 teaspoon thyme

1 teaspoon parsley

1 tablespoon brown sugar

⅛ teaspoon red pepper flakes

¼ cup vodka

Salt and pepper to taste

¼ cup whipping cream

¼ cup Grana Padano cheese, grated

1. In a pot, bring chicken stock to a boil. Cook spaghetti in chicken stock instead of water, following package directions. Drain and set aside.
2. In a saucepan, heat oil, then add onion, bell pepper, and garlic. Sauté onion over medium heat until it is clear. Add tomato paste, diced tomatoes, basil, oregano, thyme, parsley, brown sugar, red pepper flakes, vodka, salt, and pepper. Simmer on low heat for 15–20 minutes. To finish, stir in whipping cream and remove from heat.
3. Place cooked pasta in a large bowl. Add warm sauce on top, then sprinkle with Grana Padano and serve.

ALCOHOL CONTENT:

SUGGESTED PAIRING: Caesar salad

Drink Pairing: *Chianti*

To beer! A high and mighty liquor. **Julius Caesar**

> **Tipsy Trivia**
> Chianti comes in two categories: *normale* and *riserva*. *Riserva* has been aged longer and has a higher content of alcohol. *Bella!*

Devil's Got My Baby Vodka Rosemary Chicken

Call me what you like, only give me some vodka.
—RUSSIAN PROVERB

SERVES 2

2 boneless chicken breasts

2 teaspoons fresh rosemary leaves, finely minced

2 cloves garlic, minced

2 tablespoons lemon tea vodka

1 tablespoon olive oil

Salt and pepper, to taste

1. Preheat oven to 350°F.
2. Place chicken in a baking dish. In a separate bowl, combine rosemary leaves, garlic, and lemon tea vodka. Lift skin from chicken and insert mixture under chicken skin. Drizzle olive oil on top of breasts and sprinkle salt and pepper to taste.
3. Cook for 30 minutes or until chicken is cooked through.

ALCOHOL CONTENT:

SUGGESTED PAIRING: French green beans

Drink Pairing: *Cape Codder*	
1 glass ice 1½ ounces vodka 3 ounces cranberry juice 1 lime wedge, for garnish	Put ice in a glass. Pour vodka and cranberry juice over the ice. Stir. Garnish with lime wedge.

May you have the hindsight to know where you've been, the foresight to know where you are going, and the insight to know when you have gone too far. **Irish toast**

> **Tipsy Trivia**
> The average Russian drinks over three and a half gallons of vodka a year. *Nostrovia!*

High Ball Cinnamon Whiskey Chicken

We borrowed golf from Scotland as we borrowed whiskey. Not because it is Scottish, but because it is good.

—HORACE HUTCHINSON

SERVES 2

2 boneless, skinless chicken breasts

1 jalapeño pepper, seeded and chopped

1 green onion, chopped

1 teaspoon allspice

½ teaspoon nutmeg

½ teaspoon salt

1 tablespoon ginger vodka

¼ teaspoon black pepper

1 garlic clove, chopped

1 tablespoon cinnamon whiskey

2 tablespoons peanut oil

1. Place chicken breasts in a shallow dish. Combine jalapeño, green onion, allspice, nutmeg, salt, ginger vodka, black pepper, garlic, and whiskey into a food processor to form a paste. Add oil and blend until smooth.
2. Rub marinade on both sides of chicken and let stand in refrigerator for 30 minutes.
3. Preheat grill to medium-high heat. Grill chicken breasts for approximately 4–6 minutes per side, until no longer pink and juices run clear. Serve.

ALCOHOL CONTENT:

SUGGESTED PAIRING: Mashed potatoes

Drink Pairing: *Fire Ball*	
1 ounce cinnamon schnapps Dash of hot sauce	Pour cinnamon schnapps into a shot glass, add hot sauce, and mix well.

To highballs and high spirits. **Author unknown**

> **Tipsy Trivia**
> Recipe for a highball. Mix any spirit with ice and soda water in an old-fashioned jelly glass. Or you could use a highball glass to be conventional.

Samurai Sword Sake Salmon

I'd prefer to have a full bottle in front of me than a full frontal lobotomy.
—**FRANK NICHOLSON, ATTRIBUTED**

SERVES 2

½ cup unfiltered sake

¼ cup low-sodium soy sauce

2 tablespoons ginger vodka

2 cloves garlic, grated

¼ teaspoon red chili pepper flakes

2 tablespoons sugar

2 salmon fillets

2 tablespoons olive oil

½ cup chicken or seafood stock

1 tablespoon unsulphured molasses

½ cup whipping cream

2 tablespoons unsalted butter

1. In a resealable plastic bag combine sake, soy sauce, ginger vodka, garlic, red pepper flakes, and sugar. Add salmon to bag, seal, and marinate in the refrigerator for 2 hours. (You may want to place the plastic bag in a container to prevent leaking.)

2. In a large skillet, heat the olive oil to hot. Remove the salmon fillets from the plastic bag (reserving the marinade for later use) and pat them dry using clean paper towels. Place them gently in the hot oil with the skin on the bottom of the skillet. Sauté until the skin is a deep golden brown and crispy. Gently turn them over and cook 3–5 minutes, depending on thickness of salmon, or to desired doneness. Remove them from the pan and keep warm.

3. Remove the pan from the heat and pour the remaining marinade into the skillet. Return the pan to the heat, add stock and molasses, and simmer gently until thickened. Whisk in the whipping cream and bring back to a simmer. Remove from the heat, whisk in the butter, and serve with the salmon.

ALCOHOL CONTENT:

SUGGESTED PAIRING: Asparagus

Drink Pairing: *Chablis*

Thank God for the Irish; how else would we toast? **Author unknown**

> **Tipsy Trivia**
> Sake is a natural fermented beverage made from water, rice, and *koji* (a beneficial mold that allows the rice to ferment.)

Last Call Long Island Iced Tea Chicken

Be wary of strong drink. It can make you shoot at tax collectors . . . and miss.
—**ROBERT HEINLEIN**

SERVES 2

2 tablespoons vodka

2 tablespoons gin

2 tablespoons rum

2 tablespoons triple sec

2 tablespoons tequila

2 tablespoons whiskey

1 ounce sweet-and-sour mix

Splash of cola

2 boneless, skinless chicken breasts

2 tablespoons olive oil

½ cup chicken stock

¼ teaspoon salt

¼ teaspoon red pepper flakes

¼ cup whipping cream

1 tablespoon unsalted butter

1. In a resealable plastic bag, combine all liquors, sweet-and-sour mix, and cola. Add chicken and seal, ensuring chicken is coated with marinade. Marinate in the refrigerator for 2 hours.
2. Take the chicken out of the plastic bag (reserving the marinade) and pat the chicken dry. Heat the oil in a large skillet and sauté the breasts for approximately 4–6 minutes per side, until golden. Remove the chicken from the pan and keep warm.
3. Pour the reserved marinade into the pan along with the chicken stock. Bring liquid to a simmer while whisking up all the caramelized bits from the bottom of the pan.
4. Whisk in the salt and red pepper flakes and simmer until thickened. Whisk in the cream and bring back to a simmer. Remove pan from heat. Whisk in butter. Serve sauce over the warm chicken.

ALCOHOL CONTENT:

SUGGESTED PAIRING: Rosemary potatoes

Drink Pairing: *Long Island Ice Tea*	
1½ ounces vodka 1½ ounces tequila 1½ ounces rum 1½ ounces gin 1½ ounces triple sec 2 ounces cola 1 cup ice 1 lemon wedge, for garnish	Add vodka, tequila, rum, gin, triple sec, and cola to a cocktail shaker. Shake vigorously until frothy. Pour shaker contents into glass of ice and garnish with lemon wedge.

Tipsy Trivia
The Long Island iced tea, a deceptively powerful drink that has led to many unexpected evening adventures, was invented by Robert (Rosebud) Butt in the town of Babylon, Long Island, New York.

To waking up on a bed and not under it. **Author unknown**

Straight-Up Gin Shrimp

Too much of anything is bad, but too much of good whiskey is barely enough.
—MARK TWAIN

SERVES 6

2 tablespoons olive oil

½ cup onion, chopped

1 pound shrimp, raw, peeled

1 tablespoon sugar

¼ teaspoon salt

¼ cup gin

2 tablespoons ginger vodka

1 tablespoon cilantro, finely chopped

1. Heat pan and add olive oil over medium-low heat. Add onion and sauté until clear.
2. Mix in shrimp. Cook shrimp until pink, then remove them from the pan and keep them warm.
3. In the same pan, add the sugar, salt, gin, and ginger vodka and simmer until thickened. Add the shrimp back into the pan. Remove from heat and sprinkle the chopped cilantro on top. Serve.

ALCOHOL CONTENT:

SUGGESTED PAIRING: Orzo

Drink Pairing: *Gin Blossom*	
1 cup ice ¾ ounce gin ¾ ounce vodka 3 ounces cranberry juice 3 ounces orange juice	In a Collins glass, add ice, gin, and vodka. Add orange juice and cranberry juice and serve without mixing.

Here's to our hostess, considerate and sweet; her wit is endless, but when do we eat? **Author unknown**

> **Tipsy Trivia**
> Some towns were so convinced that alcohol was the source of all crime that they actually sold their jails on the eve of Prohibition. You have to admire that level of belief.

Raise Your Glass to Embracing Change!

Midnight Bourbon Baby Back Ribs

If you are young and you drink a great deal it will spoil your health, slow your mind, make you fat—in other words, turn you into an adult.

—**P. J. O'ROURKE**

SERVES 2

1 pound baby back pork ribs

Salt and pepper

1 tablespoon chili powder

1 tablespoon paprika

1 tablespoon garlic powder

1 teaspoon cumin

1 cup purchased plain barbecue sauce

¼ cup onion chopped

2 tablespoons bourbon

1. Preheat grill to medium-low.
2. Place the ribs on a work surface and salt and pepper to taste. In a bowl, mix the chili powder, paprika, garlic powder, and cumin. Pat the dry rub over the ribs and place on the grill.
3. Cook ribs on grill until done, keeping them out of direct heat. In general, ribs take 2–2½ hours to cook. Keep the temperature around 225°F and turn the ribs occasionally throughout the grilling process.
4. In a saucepan on low heat, mix the barbecue sauce, onion, and bourbon. Simmer for 3 minutes. Apply to ribs 7 minutes before the meat is done cooking.

ALCOHOL CONTENT:

SUGGESTED PAIRING: Macaroni salad

Drink Pairing: *Black and Tan*	
Half glass light ale (number of ounces depends on size of glass) Half glass of stout (number of ounces depends on size of glass)	Fill a glass half full with light ale. Fill the rest of the glass with stout ale by pouring it over a spoon to layer it.

Tipsy Trivia
Bourbon, like champagne and tequila, takes its name from the location where it was invented—in this case, Bourbon County, Kentucky.

When we drink, we get drunk. When we get drunk, we fall asleep. When we fall asleep, we commit no sin, when we commit no sin, we go to heaven. So, let's all get drunk, and go to heaven! **Author Unknown**

Chillin' Whiskey Pork Chops

Never cry over spilt milk. It could've been whiskey.
—**"PAPPY" MAVERICK**

SERVES 4

2 center-cut pork chops

2 tablespoons vegetable oil

8 ounces mushrooms, sliced

⅓ cup maple syrup

1 cup beef broth

½ cup whiskey

2 teaspoons dry mustard

1 tablespoon fresh parsley, chopped

1 onion, diced

Salt and pepper, to taste

1 cup sour cream

1. In a large skillet, lightly brown chops in oil over medium heat.
2. In a bowl combine mushrooms, maple syrup, broth, whiskey, mustard, parsley, onions, salt, and pepper.
3. Drizzle mushroom sauce over pork chops. Cover and simmer for 50 minutes or until pork chops are tender. Add sour cream and heat pork chops up to serving temperature, then remove from heat. Serve.

ALCOHOL CONTENT:

SUGGESTED PAIRING: Applesauce

Drink Pairing: *Rusty Nail*	
1½ ounces scotch ½ ounce Drambuie 1 twist lemon peel	Pour Scotch and Drambuie into a glass. Mix well. Garnish with the lemon twist.

May our friends who are coming arrive soon, may our friends who have arrived have a drink, and may our friends who are drunk go to sleep.
Author unknown

Tipsy Trivia
There are two ways to spell "whiskey." You can spell it like the Scots and Canadians: "whisky." Or you can spell it like the Irish and Americans: "whiskey." However, there is only one way to spell "hung over."

Merry Red Snapper with Mango Rum

Not all chemicals are bad. Without chemicals such as hydrogen and oxygen, for example, there would be no way to make water, a vital ingredient in beer.

—DAVE BARRY

SERVES 2

2 tablespoons mango rum

3 teaspoons cilantro, chopped

1 lime, juiced

2 tablespoons olive oil

2 5-ounce red snapper fillets

Salt and pepper to taste

1. Combine rum, cilantro, lime juice, and olive oil into bowl and mix.
2. Season fish with salt and pepper to taste. Coat the snapper fillets with the marinade, reserving a little marinade for dressing if desired. Depending on how you would like to grill the fish, follow the directions below.
3. Preheat grill to medium. Oil aluminum foil and wrap fillets. Place fillets on the grill, away from direct heat. Grill until fish is cooked thoroughly, about 10 minutes. Serve using reserved marinade as dressing, if desired.

ALCOHOL CONTENT:

SUGGESTED PAIRING: Baked potato

Drink Pairing: *Moselle*

Arrgh. Drink ye rum! **Pirate toast**

Tipsy Trivia
August 16 is National Rum Day, not to be confused with September 19, which is Official Talk-Like-a-Pirate Day.

Raise Your Glass to Wisdom!

Dancing Tilapia in Rum Butter Sauce

I drink therefore I am.
—W. C. FIELDS

SERVES 2

2 tablespoons butter

2 tilapia fillets

Salt and pepper to taste

2 tablespoons olive oil

1 shallot, grated

1 teaspoon garlic powder

1 tablespoon rum

1 tablespoon lemon tea vodka

1 tablespoon orange vodka

2 teaspoons honey

1. In a large skillet melt butter over medium heat. Heat the butter until browned and foamy. Add tilapia, season with salt and pepper, and cook 4 minutes on each side until fish flakes easily with fork and is cooked through. Move the fish to a platter and keep warm.
2. In the same skillet, add olive oil, shallot, and garlic powder, cooking over medium heat until shallots are translucent. Remove the pan from the heat. Add the liquors to the pan and return it to the heat. Bring the mixture back to a low simmer and cook for two minutes.
3. Whisking gently, incorporate the honey throughout the sauce and remove from the heat. Add the fish back to the pan and baste with the sauce. Serve warm.

ALCOHOL CONTENT:

SUGGESTED PAIRING: Wild rice

Drink Pairing: *Piña Colada*	
4 ounces fresh pineapple juice 3 ounces rum 2 ounces coconut cream 2 cups crushed ice 1 slice fresh pineapple for garnish	Place all of the ingredients into a blender (except pineapple garnish) and blend until smooth. Pour into a glass and serve. Garnish with a slice of fresh pineapple.

May you travel the world but remember how to get home. **Author unknown**

Tipsy Trivia
The piña colada is the official drink of Puerto Rico.
Vamanos!

Raise Your Glass to Being in the Moment!

Play-It-Again Gin Scallops

I'll stick with gin. Champagne is just ginger ale that knows somebody.
—**HAWKEYE PIERCE ON M*A*S*H**

SERVES 2

8 large sea scallops (fresh scallops are best)

Salt and pepper to taste

2 tablespoons olive oil

1 tablespoon lime juice

1 tablespoon gin (you can also use lime-flavored gin for extra lime taste)

2 tablespoons butter

2 tablespoons chives

1. Sprinkle scallops with salt and pepper and let rest for a couple of minutes. In a skillet on medium-low heat, add oil. When hot, place scallops in the skillet. Sear quickly 1 minute or so each side. Remove scallops and place on clean plate.
2. In the same skillet add lime juice and gin. Bring to a boil and reduce the sauce by half. Turn off the heat and whisk in butter, then add the scallops to the skillet with the chives. Let sit for 30–60 seconds. Do not overcook scallops. Serve.

ALCOHOL CONTENT:

SUGGESTED PAIRING: Risotto

Drink Pairing: *Gin and Tonic*	
1 cup ice 2 ounces gin 5 ounces tonic water 1 lime wedge	Place ice in a highball glass. Pour the gin and tonic water into the glass. Stir well. Garnish with the lime wedge.

A man hath no better thing under the sun than to eat, and to drink, and to be merry. **Ecclesiastes 8:15**

> **Tipsy Trivia**
> The tonic in a gin and tonic contains quinine and can help prevent malaria. So stock up before you go camping.

Raise Your Glass to Loving Life!

Feeling Good Vodka Enchiladas

And smoking weed kills your brain cells, not like getting drunk which only hurts the liver, and you got two of them.

—**EARL J. HICKEY**

SERVES 6

Enchiladas

1 can diced Rotel tomatoes with green chilies

1 can cream of chicken soup

4 boneless, skinless chicken breasts, cooked and shredded

8 ounces sour cream

12 tortillas

12 ounces shredded Cheddar cheese, divided

1. Preheat oven to 375°F.
2. In a bowl, prepare the enchiladas. Mix Rotel tomatoes and soup. Pour ¼ of the mixture into a 9" × 13" inch baking pan to provide a thin coating.
3. In another bowl, mix the chicken and sour cream. Spoon chicken mixture onto each tortilla. Place ½ ounce Cheddar on top of chicken mixture in each tortilla, setting the remaining cheese aside.
4. Roll up each tortilla. Place all the tortillas in the baking pan, spooning in soup mixture between them to keep them from sticking to one another. Cover with the remaining soup mixture. Spread remaining cheese evenly on top of all the tortillas.
5. Bake for 30–45 minutes until cheese and mixture are bubbling.

(See following page for salsa recipe)

Tipsy Trivia
Vodka was once used in Poland as an aftershave.

Raise Your Glass to Encouragement!

Salsa

1 14.5-ounce can diced tomatoes

2 bunches green onions, chopped (both white and green portions)

1 garlic clove, minced

2 tablespoons fresh cilantro, minced

¼ teaspoon salt

1 jalapeño, seeded and chopped

1 tablespoon lime juice

2 tablespoons mango vodka

1. Make the salsa as the enchiladas cook. Blend all salsa ingredients in a food processor until desired consistency. Allow salsa to stand for at least 30 minutes to allow the flavors to enhance. Serve with enchiladas.

ALCOHOL CONTENT:

SUGGESTED PAIRING: Black beans

Drink Pairing: *Jalapeño Cilantro Margarita*	
1 cup ice 1 ounce tequila 1 ounce triple sec 3 ounces lime juice 1 teaspoon sugar ¼ teaspoon salt 2 jalapeño peppers, divided 1 sprig cilantro, for garnish	Fill a shaker with ice and add tequila, triple sec, lime juice, sugar, and salt. Shake well. Muddle 1 jalapeño pepper and cilantro at bottom of chilled margarita glass and strain mixture into it. Garnish with remaining jalapeño pepper.

May the lilt of Irish laughter lighten every load. May the mist of Irish magic shorten every road. . . . And may all your friends remember all the favors you are owed! **Irish toast**

Island Getaway Cherry Rum and Balsamic Salmon

Auntie Hanna laced her tea with rum, because it was only once a year.
—**DYLAN THOMAS,** *A CHILD'S CHRISTMAS IN WALES*

SERVES 2

2 salmon fillets (4 ounces each)

Sea salt and pepper to taste

¼ cup balsamic dressing

1 tablespoon cherry rum

1 teaspoon garlic powder

2 tablespoons olive oil

Additional oil for grilling

1. Season the salmon with salt and pepper and set aside.
2. In a bowl, mix balsamic dressing, cherry rum, garlic powder, and olive oil. Coat salmon with mixture.
3. Preheat grill on medium. Wrap fish in oiled aluminum foil and place on the grill away from direct heat. Grill until fish is cooked thoroughly, about 10 minutes. Serve.

ALCOHOL CONTENT:

SUGGESTED PAIRING: Polenta

Drink Pairing: *Cherry Cola*	
1 glass filled with ice 1½ ounces rum 4 ounces cherry cola 1 lime twist 1 lime wedge	In a highball or Collins glass filled with ice, add rum, cherry cola, and twist of lime. Garnish with the lime wedge.

Life is uncertain. Eat dessert first. **Ernestine Ulmer**

Tipsy Trivia
Paul Revere, John Adams, and John Hancock were all rum enthusiasts. This makes the Massachusetts ban on Happy Hour even more confusing.

Raise Your Glass to Taking Risks!

Five O'Clock Beer Flank Steak

24 hours in a day, 24 beers in a case. Coincidence?
—STEPHEN WRIGHT

SERVES 8

1 bottle beer

3 garlic cloves, chopped

1 cup onion, chopped

½ teaspoon salt

1 teaspoon pepper

2 pounds flank steak

1. Mix beer, garlic, onion, salt, and pepper and pour into a resealable plastic bag. Add flank steak and refrigerate for 4 hours or longer.
2. Preheat grill to medium-high. Grill meat over medium-high heat for 5–6 minutes per side or until desired doneness.
3. Let meat stand for 10 minutes before slicing on a diagonal. Serve.

ALCOHOL CONTENT:

SUGGESTED PAIRING: Potatoes

Drink Pairing: *Pilsner*

To a long summer with fast friends. **Author unknown**

Tipsy Trivia
Pilsner takes its name from the city of Pilsen, Bohemia. It's the beer that made Pilsen famous. Kind of like Old Milwaukee.

Pub Scallops with White Wine Sauce

The church is near, but the road is icy. The bar is far, but we will walk carefully.
—**RUSSIAN PROVERB**

SERVES 2–4

1 pound small sea scallops

1 tablespoon olive oil

Salt and pepper, to taste

½ cup chicken broth

1 garlic clove, minced

1 tablespoon lemon tea vodka

¼ cup white wine

1 tablespoon onion, finely chopped

3 tablespoons butter, room temperature

1. Preheat the oven broiler.
2. Coat scallops lightly with olive oil and salt and pepper.
3. Cook the scallops in a large skillet over medium-high heat, for 2–3 minutes on each side or until opaque, with a little browning on the sides. Remove from the skillet and keep warm.
4. In the same skillet, combine the chicken broth, garlic, lemon tea vodka, wine, and onion. Cook until most of the liquid has been evaporated, and only 2–3 tablespoons are left. Remove from heat and whisk in the butter.
5. Pour sauce over scallops. Serve.

ALCOHOL CONTENT:

SUGGESTED PAIRING: Spinach

Drink Pairing: *Chablis*

Stir the eggnog, lift the toddy, Happy New Year, everybody. **Phyllis McGinley**

Tipsy Trivia
Because it's easier than calling it the windy-twisty-pokey thing, the curled metal part of a corkscrew is called the worm.

Raise Your Glass to Innocence!

Sinful Gin Chicken Alfredo

Give a man a beer, waste an hour. Teach a man to brew, and waste a lifetime!

—BILL OWEN

SERVES 4

12 ounces penne

2 quarts chicken stock

2 tablespoons extra-virgin olive oil

4 boneless, skinless chicken breasts, cut into cubes

1 cup whipping cream

1½ cups finely grated Parmesan cheese

1 teaspoon basil

½ teaspoon garlic powder

1 teaspoon parsley flakes

Salt and pepper to taste

2 tablespoons gin

1 egg yolk, beaten

1. Cook penne in chicken stock to desired doneness. Drain and set aside.
2. Heat olive oil in a saucepan over medium heat.
3. Add chicken and cook until it's not pink inside. Remove from heat and set aside.
4. In a separate saucepan, heat cream over medium heat. Slowly blend in cheese until melted. Continue to stir slowly while adding spices and gin. Blend in egg yolk to thicken.
5. Place chicken over penne and spoon sauce on top. Serve.

ALCOHOL CONTENT:

SUGGESTED PAIRING: **Salad**

Drink Pairing: *Martini*	
2½ ounces gin ¼ ounce dry vermouth 2 green olives Shaker filled with ice cubes	Place ice cubes in a shaker. Pour in the gin and vermouth. Shake well. Strain and pour into a martini glass. Garnish with olives.

May your mornings bring joy and your evenings bring peace. May your troubles grow less as your blessings increase! **Irish toast**

Tipsy Trivia
Gin is infused with juniper berries, which are a kind of pine cone. This gives gin its piney flavor. Merry Christmas!

Bartender Garlic and Rum Roast Pork

Time is never wasted when you're wasted all the time.
—CATHERINE ZANDONELLA

SERVES 6

3 pounds pork loin

4 garlic cloves, peeled and chopped

1 teaspoon salt

1 teaspoon black pepper

½ cup rum

½ cup brown sugar

1½ cups chicken broth

¼ cup ginger vodka

2 limes, juiced

1. Preheat oven to 350°F. Season pork by rubbing it with garlic, salt, and pepper. Set aside.
2. In a bowl, combine rum, brown sugar, chicken broth, ginger vodka, and lime juice. Pour ½ liquid in roasting pan. Place pork in pan and pour remaining mixture over top.
3. Bake for 60–90 minutes (roughly 20–30 minutes per pound) turning halfway through cook time. Slice and serve.

ALCOHOL CONTENT:

SUGGESTED PAIRING: Roasted potatoes

Drink Pairing: *Strawberry Daiquiri*	
2 ounces white rum 1 ounce lime juice ½ ounce triple sec ½ teaspoon powdered sugar 1 cup ice 1 cup strawberries (fresh or frozen)	Mix all ingredients in a blender quickly at high speed until combined. Pour into a glass.

Yo-ho-ho and a bottle of rum! **Robert Louis Stevenson,** *Treasure Island*

> **Tipsy Trivia**
> **Remember to use heavier, darker rums for sipping and save light rums for mixed drinks.**

Raise Your Glass to New Ideas!

Wasted Beer Beef Stew

Beer is proof that God loves us and wants us to be happy.

—BENJAMIN FRANKLIN

SERVES 6

2 tablespoons olive oil

1½ pounds beef stew meat, cut into 1" cubes

½ cup onions, chopped

4 cups beef stock

4 cloves garlic, chopped

1 bottle beer

2 cups carrots, cut in 1" pieces

8 red potatoes, cut in 1" pieces

1 teaspoon salt

1 teaspoon pepper

1. In a large pot, heat olive oil over medium-high heat. Cook beef until nicely browned on all sides.
2. Add onions and sauté until tender. Add beef stock, garlic, beer, carrots, potatoes, salt, and pepper.
3. Cover and simmer for 2½ hours or until potatoes are tender, stirring occasionally. Serve.

ALCOHOL CONTENT:

SUGGESTED PAIRING: Biscuits

Drink Pairing: *Light ale*	
2 ounces white rum 1 ounce lime juice ½ ounce triple sec ½ teaspoon powdered sugar 1 cup ice 1 cup strawberries (fresh or frozen)	Mix all ingredients in a blender quickly at high speed until combined. Pour into a glass.

Give me a woman who loves beer and I will conquer the world. **Kaiser Wilhelm**

Cooking with Beer
Beer flavor varies widely from lagers to stouts. Try a variety of beers in your recipes to find the beer that works best.

Shooters BBQ Rum Salmon

Alcohol is necessary for a man so that he can have a good opinion of himself, undisturbed by the facts.

—FINLEY PETER DUNNE

SERVES 4

½ of a 9-ounce bottle plain barbecue sauce

1 tablespoon olive oil

½ cup dark rum

¼ cup onion, chopped

1 tablespoon garlic powder

4 5-ounce salmon fillets

Sprinkling of salt

1. Preheat grill to medium-high.
2. Add barbecue sauce and rum in a saucepan over medium heat and heat through.
3. In a skillet on medium heat, add olive oil and sauté onions and garlic for a few minutes, until the onions are soft.
4. Add onions and garlic to the barbecue saucepan, and bring to a boil. Reduce heat and simmer for 5 minutes. Remove from heat and let it cool completely.
5. Set ⅓ barbecue sauce aside for dipping and coat salmon with the remainder. Put fish in the refrigerator and let it marinate for 1–2 hours, less if you're in a hurry.
6. Sprinkle the salmon with a pinch of salt. Oil aluminum foil and wrap salmon. Grill until fish is cooked thoroughly, about 10 minutes.
7. Remove fish from the grill. Pour barbecue sauce over the fish before serving.

ALCOHOL CONTENT:

SUGGESTED PAIRING: Potato salad

Drink Pairing: *Chardonnay*

To my best mirror, an old friend. **George Herbert**

Luau Lime Gin Mahi Mahi

I spent a lot of my money on booze, birds, and fast cars. The rest I just squandered.
—GEORGE BEST

SERVES 2

2 mahi mahi fillets (6 ounces each)

¼ teaspoon salt

¼ teaspoon freshly ground black pepper

Juice of 1½ limes

2 tablespoons orange vodka

2 tablespoons lemon tea vodka

2 tablespoons lime gin

2 tablespoons ginger vodka

1 garlic clove, minced

¼ cup olive oil

1 tablespoon cilantro, chopped

2 tablespoons butter

1. Season the mahi mahi fillets with salt and pepper. Set aside.
2. In a bowl, mix lime juice, orange vodka, lemon tea vodka, lime gin, ginger vodka, and garlic. Apply ⅓ of the marinade mixture over the fillets. Put the rest of the marinade aside to use for sauce. Let mahi mahi soak in marinade for 10 minutes before placing on grill.
3. Preheat grill on medium. Wrap fish in oiled aluminum foil and place on grill. Grill until fish is cooked thoroughly, about 10 minutes.
4. In a saucepan on low heat melt butter. Add the rest of the marinade and simmer on low heat. Add the cilantro. Serve over grilled fish.

ALCOHOL CONTENT:

SUGGESTED PAIRING: Green beans with toasted almonds

Drink Pairing: *Sauvignon Blanc*

To doing what we love and loving what we do. **Traditional toast**

> **Tipsy Trivia**
> The proof number on alcohol is twice the percentage of alcohol in the drink. So 80 proof gin is 40 percent alcohol and Bacardi 151 is, well, you get the idea.

Frolicking Rum Curry Chicken

The three-martini lunch is the epitome of American efficiency. Where else can you get an earful, a bellyful, and a snootful at the same time?

—GERALD R. FORD

SERVES 4–6

1 tablespoon curry powder

1 cup coconut milk

1 tablespoon rum

½ hot pepper, seeded and chopped (optional)

1 tablespoon sesame oil

1 tablespoon olive oil

4 boneless, skinless chicken breasts, cut into 1" pieces

2 garlic cloves, chopped fine

Salt and pepper, to taste

4½ cups chicken stock

2 cups rice

2 scallions, chopped

1. In a bowl, combine curry powder, coconut milk, rum, and hot pepper (if desired). Set aside.
2. Heat sesame and olive oils in large pan over medium-high heat. Add chicken and cook until all the chicken is browned. Add garlic. Pour coconut mixture over chicken and reduce heat to a simmer for about 15 minutes. Add salt and pepper to taste. While chicken cooks, bring 4½ cups chicken stock to a boil in a large pot. Add rice and stir. Reduce heat to simmer and cover, cooking according to directions on rice package.
3. Serve chicken with sauce over rice and sprinkle scallions on top.

ALCOHOL CONTENT:

SUGGESTED FOOD PAIRING: Raita

Drink Pairing: *Chardonnay*

Today it is our pleasure to be drunk. **Henry Fielding**

Tipsy Trivia

Inspectors in the eighteenth century would "prove" the amount of alcohol in a spirit by mixing it with gunpowder and lighting it on fire. If it caught fire it was 100 percent proven or "100 proof." It took a 50-percent alcohol concentration for the concoction to catch fire, so 100 proof became the same as 50 percent alcohol.

Raise Your Glass to Belief!

Fiesta Tequila Lamb Chops with Mango Salsa

There were years when I was a beer and tequila guy; then I got real fat. And then I found that you could actually go on a diet and drink Scotch. Then I got hooked on scotch; then everything else just tastes wrong.

—RON WHITE

SERVES 4

¼ cup lime juice

¼ cup tequila

1 tablespoon garlic, minced

¼ cup olive oil

1 teaspoon salt

½ teaspoon pepper

4 lamb chops, 1" thick

Salsa

1 (14.5-ounce) can diced tomatoes

2 bunches green onions, chop white and green portions

1 garlic clove, minced

2 tablespoons fresh cilantro, minced

1 teaspoon jalapeño, seeded and chopped

1 tablespoon lime juice

2 tablespoons mango vodka

1. Mix lime juice, tequila, garlic, oil, salt, and pepper in a resealable plastic bag. Add lamb chops and marinate in the refrigerator for a minimum of 2 hours.
2. Make salsa by combining all salsa ingredients in a food processor and pulsing until desired consistency is reached. Let flavors mingle for at least ½ hour before serving.
3. Preheat your grill on high heat. Oil the grill grates. Place lamb chops on grill with the lid open. Grill for 7–8 minutes on each side until desired doneness. Remove from the grill. Let stand 5 minutes.
4. As lamb chops stand, stir together the salsa ingredients.
5. Spoon salsa over lamp chops and serve.

ALCOHOL CONTENT:

SUGGESTED PAIRING: Risotto

Drink Pairing: *Cabernet Sauvignon*

May you be in heaven a full half hour before the devil knows you're dead.
Various attributions

Stumbling Chicken Breasts with Champagne Sauce

The problem with the world is that everyone is a few drinks behind.

—HUMPHREY BOGART

SERVES 4

2 tablespoons olive oil

4 boneless, skinless chicken breasts

2 tablespoons butter

¾ cup diced mushrooms, optional

¼ cup shallots, minced

1 cup whipping cream

1 cup champagne

1 cup chicken broth

Salt, to taste

1. Heat oil over medium-high heat in a large pan. Cook chicken breasts in the oil until both sides are lightly browned. Remove chicken and set aside.
2. In the same pan, add butter, mushrooms, and shallots. Cook until shallots are brown.
3. In bowl, mix cream, champagne, and chicken broth and pour into pan. Bring to a boil and then reduce heat to medium. Return chicken to the pan. Continue to cook until chicken is cooked through. Salt to taste.
4. Serve.

ALCOHOL CONTENT:

SUGGESTED PAIRING: Rice or noodles

Drink Pairing: *Rosé*

Let us toast toast! Without it we'd be eating caviar with our fingers.
Author unknown

Tipsy Trivia
When the drafters of the U.S. Constitution finally got out of their meetings they had a party to remember. They were billed for 144 bottles of Madeira, claret, whiskey, and port, plus twenty bottles of hard cider and beer. Not to mention the seven bowls of alcoholic punch.

Umbrella Mussels with Beer

A fine beer may be judged with only one sip, but it's better to be thoroughly sure.
—CZECH PROVERB

SERVES 4

2–4 pounds of mussels

1 bottle beer

½ teaspoon parsley

½ teaspoon oregano

½ teaspoon basil

½ teaspoon thyme

3 cloves garlic, finely chopped

½ teaspoon salt

1. Wash and scrub mussels under cold water. Dispose of all broken or dead mussels. In a large pot over medium heat, add beer, herbs, garlic, and salt. Simmer 3–5 minutes. Add mussels, cover the pot, and increase to high heat. Cook until mussels open. Discard any unopened mussels.
2. Place mussels and broth in a bowl and serve.

ALCOHOL CONTENT:

SUGGESTED PAIRING: Buttery, crusty, grilled baguette

Drink Pairing: *Moselle*

Blessed are the cheese makers, for they shall inherit the earth.
Monty Python, *Life of Brian*

Tipsy Trivia
It is illegal to serve beer and pretzels together in North Dakota. It must have been a defense against invasion by the Bavarians.

LOL Lemon Tea and Dill Tilapia

I distrust camels and anyone else who can go a week without a drink.

—JOE E. LEWIS

SERVES 2

2 tablespoons olive oil

2 tablespoons lemon tea vodka

1 teaspoon garlic powder

3 tablespoons dill, fresh

¼ teaspoon salt

2 tilapia fillets

½ cup orange juice

1 tablespoon lemon vodka

3 tablespoons whipping cream

1 tablespoon butter

Sprinkle of salt

1. In a large, resealable plastic bag, combine oil, vodka, garlic powder, dill, and salt. Massage gently to combine all ingredients. Unseal the bag and carefully lay each piece of fish inside, ensuring fish is thoroughly coated with marinade. Reseal the bag and marinate in the refrigerator for 1 hour.
2. Preheat grill to medium-high. Wrap each fillet in oiled aluminum foil. Reserve the marinade for later use. Place fillets on grill and cook 6–8 minutes per side until done and the fish is flaky.
3. Pour the leftover marinade into a skillet. Add orange juice and lemon vodka. Bring to a simmer, whisking frequently until thickened. Whisk in the cream. Remove from heat and blend in butter and salt. Pour over the grilled fish. Serve.

ALCOHOL CONTENT:

SUGGESTED PAIRING: Brown rice

Drink Pairing: *Chardonnay*

It is better to spend money like there is no tomorrow than to spend tonight like there is no money. **Unknown author**

> **Tipsy Trivia**
> **Flavored rums and vodkas are 5 to 10 percent weaker than their unflavored siblings, which is a fine rationalization to use them freely.**

Make It a Double Vodka Pork Chops

I drink to forget I drink.

—JOE E. LEWIS

SERVES 2

¼ cup orange juice

1 tablespoon orange vodka

1 tablespoon ginger vodka

2 tablespoons honey

4 tablespoons olive oil, divided

½ teaspoon garlic powder

½ teaspoon salt

¼ teaspoon freshly ground black pepper

4 lean pork chops

¼ cup whipping cream

1 tablespoon unsalted butter

1. In a resealable plastic bag, add orange juice, vodkas, honey, 2 tablespoons olive oil, garlic powder, salt, black pepper, and pork chops. Marinate for 1–2 hours.

2. In a pan, heat 2 tablespoons of olive oil. Add pork chops, cooking at medium heat for about 4 minutes on each side. Remove from the pan and keep warm.

3. In the same pan, add sauce from the plastic bag and simmer until thickened, gently scraping off the stuck-on bits with a whisk. Whisk in the cream, bringing the sauce back to a simmer. Remove from heat and whisk in the butter along with any juices from the resting pork chops. Pour the sauce over the warm pork chops.

ALCOHOL CONTENT:

SUGGESTED PAIRING: Swiss chard

Drink Pairing: *Sex on the Beach*	
1½ ounces vodka ½ ounce peach schnapps 2 ounces cranberry juice 2 ounces orange juice	Place ice in a highball glass. Combine vodka and peach schnapps in a glass. Pour in cranberry juice and orange juice. Stir until mixed.

Health to the men, and may the women live forever. **Various attributions**

Tipsy Trivia

The seventeenth-century English king, William III, liked his punch. He liked it so much that at his parties he served 1200 gallons of brandy in a pool-sized punch bowl. The bartender (boat tender?) would row around filling guests' cups.

Biker Bar Beer Steaks

I would kill everyone in this room for a drop of sweet beer.
—**HOMER SIMPSON**

SERVES 2

¼ cup lemon tea vodka

1 beer, your choice

¼ teaspoon salt

¼ teaspoon freshly ground black pepper

2 steaks, your choice

½ cup beef broth

1 tablespoon honey

1 teaspoon vanilla

1 tablespoon fig jam

½ cup whipping cream

2 tablespoons butter

1. In a resealable plastic bag combine vodka, beer, salt, and pepper. Put the steak in the bag to marinate in the refrigerator for 1–2 hours, turning the bag over from time to time to shuttle the flavors all through the steak.
2. Preheat grill on high heat.
3. Place steaks on grill. Reserve marinade. Cook for 5 minutes on each side, or until desired doneness.
4. In a medium skillet, add the reserved marinade, beef broth, honey, vanilla, and jam. Simmer until thickened. Whisk in the cream and bring back to a bubble. Remove from heat and whisk in the butter. Adjust salt to taste.
5. Pour sauce over steak and serve.

ALCOHOL CONTENT:

SUGGESTED PAIRING: Baked potatoes

Drink Pairing: *Stout*

May you always have a clean shirt, a clear conscience, and enough coins in your pocket to buy a pint! **Irish toast**

Tipsy Trivia
Barnacular: "On the rocks" means that the spirits are to be served and drunk over ice.

Surly Tequila and Shrimp

Now tequila may be the favored beverage of outlaws but that doesn't mean it gives them preferential treatment.

—**TOM ROBBINS,** *Still Life with Woodpecker*

SERVES 2

2 cups rice

2 tablespoons butter

2 tablespoons olive oil

2 teaspoons garlic powder

1 pound large shrimp, peeled and deveined

⅔ cup tequila

1 lime, juiced

3 tablespoons whipping cream

Salt and pepper, to taste

¼ cup chopped fresh cilantro

1. Cook rice according to package directions.
2. Put butter and olive oil in a skillet over medium heat. When the butter is melted, add in garlic powder and shrimp. Cook shrimp for 3 minutes or until they turn pink.
3. Remove shrimp from the pan. Remove the pan from the heat, and carefully pour in tequila and lime juice. Return the pan to the heat and simmer for 2–3 minutes. Whisk in the cream and bring back to a simmer.
4. Return the shrimp to the pan and remove the pan from the heat. Season with salt and pepper. Sprinkle fresh cilantro on top of the shrimp. Serve.

ALCOHOL CONTENT:

SUGGESTED PAIRING: Corn on the cob

Drink Pairing: *Hot Nantucket Night*	
2 jalapeños, divided 2 cranberries 2 cups ice, divided 1½ ounces tequila 1½ ounces agave nectar 1½ ounces lime juice	1. Muddle 1 jalapeño and cranberries in the bottom of a highball glass. Add 1 cup of the ice to the highball glass. 2. In a shaker, add tequila, agave nectar, lime juice, and the rest of the ice. Strain shaker over highball glass onto muddled jalapeño, cranberries, and ice. Garnish with a jalapeño pepper.

To fast cars and free parking. **Author unknown**

Singapore Sling Gin Pork Chops

I like my whiskey old and my women young.

—ERROL FLYNN

SERVES 2

2 ounces gin

Juice of 2 limes

2 garlic cloves, grated

1 packed tablespoon fresh snipped cilantro

Dash of salt and pepper

4 pork chops, 1" thick

2 tablespoons blackberry jam

3 tablespoons whipping cream

1. In a resealable plastic bag, add gin, lime juice, garlic, cilantro, salt, and pepper. Place pork chops in the bag and seal. Marinate in the refrigerator for 4 hours.
2. Preheat grill to medium-high.
3. Place pork chops on grill, reserving marinade for later use. Grill pork chops for about 5 minutes each side or until done.
4. In a small skillet, simmer the remaining pork chop marinade until it begins to thicken. Whisk in the blackberry jam until melted. Add in the cream and whisk to blend. Spoon the sauce over hot pork chops. Serve.

ALCOHOL CONTENT:

SUGGESTED PAIRING: Scalloped potatoes

Drink Pairing: *Pinot Noir*

Here's to woman! Would that we could fall into her arms without falling into her hands. **Ambrose Bierce**

> **Tipsy Trivia**
> Barnacular: "Neat" means that the spirits are to be served by themselves at room temperature with nothing added.

VSOP Brandy Steaks

It's like gambling somehow. You go out for a night of drinking and you don't know where you're going to end up the next day. It could work out good or it could be disastrous. It's like the throw of the dice.

—JIM MORRISON

SERVES 2

2 steaks (5 ounces each)

Salt and pepper, to taste, divided

3 tablespoons butter, divided

1 teaspoon lemon tea vodka

2 tablespoons of brandy

2 tablespoons Worcestershire

1 tablespoon cream

1. Preheat grill to medium-high heat. Season the steaks with salt and pepper. Place on grill and cook until desired doneness. On average, it will take 2–3 minutes per side for rare, 4–6 minutes per side for medium, and 7–9 minutes per side for well done.
2. In a skillet, melt 2 tablespoons of the butter. Add lemon vodka, brandy, and Worcestershire sauce. Whisk gently until mixture begins to thicken. Add the cream, remove from the heat, and whisk in the last tablespoon of butter. Add salt and pepper to taste. Simmer for 3–4 minutes until mixture bubbles.
3. Pour brandy sauce over steaks. Serve.

ALCOHOL CONTENT:

SUGGESTED PAIRING: Creamy mashed potatoes

Drink Pairing: *Paradise*	
1 cup ice cubes 1½ ounces gin 1 ounce apricot brandy 2 ounces orange juice	Fill a shaker with ice. Pour all ingredients over the ice. Shake to mix. Strain into your favorite cocktail glass.

To good health! **Universal**

> **Tipsy Trivia**
> Thermometers in the seventeenth century used to be filled with brandy instead of mercury, so if you drank it you'd be drunk as a skunk instead of mad as a hatter.

Raise Your Glass to Accomplishments!

CHAPTER 4

Desserts

The day has ended, the dinner has been eaten, the friends have been toasted, and the wine is gone. It's time for dessert! If there's any time of the day for eating those delicious delicacies that go straight to our waistlines, it is now.

Whether you're in the mood for apple crisp or chocolate mousse, pecan pie, or a root beer float, there is a dessert here that will end your day with a bang.

Lush Raspberry Vodka Chocolate Chip Cookies

Be careful to trust a person who does not like wine.

—KARL MARX

MAKES 24

2 cups all-purpose flour

1 teaspoon baking soda

½ teaspoon salt

1 cup butter, softened

¾ cup white sugar

¾ cup packed brown sugar

2 eggs

2 teaspoons vanilla extract

1 tablespoon raspberry vodka

2 cups chocolate chips, semisweet or dark

1 cup chopped and toasted nuts of your choice

1. Preheat oven to 350°F.
2. Combine flour, baking soda, and salt in bowl.
3. In a separate bowl, cream butter with both types of sugar. Beat in the eggs, one at a time. Stir in vanilla and vodka.
4. Slowly blend flour mixture into sugar mixture. Mix in chocolate chips and nuts. Drop by large spoonfuls onto ungreased cookie sheets.
5. Bake for about 10 minutes or until golden brown.

ALCOHOL CONTENT:

Drink Pairing: *Irish Hot Chocolate*	
2 teaspoons sugar 6–8 ounces hot brewed chocolate 1½ ounces Irish whiskey 2–4 tablespoons whipped cream, sweetened if desired (optional) 1 teaspoon Irish Mist (optional)	Put sugar, hot chocolate, and whiskey in a mug. Stir. Top with whipped cream and drizzle with Irish Mist if desired.

To good pies and strong beer. *Poor Robin's Almanack,* **1695**

> **Tipsy Trivia**
> It doesn't matter if you're drinking beer, wine, or spirits. A shot, a bottle of beer, and a glass of wine all contain the same amount of alcohol. It's all the same to a breathalyzer.

Feeling No Pain Chocolate-Vodka Banana Sundae

I should never have switched from Scotch to martinis.

—HUMPHREY BOGART'S LAST WORDS

SERVES 1

2 scoops vanilla ice cream

1–3 tablespoons chocolate syrup

1 tablespoon chocolate vodka

1 banana, sliced

¼ cup toasted nuts, your choice

2 tablespoons whipped cream

1 cherry (optional)

1. Place 2 scoops of vanilla ice cream in a bowl. Drizzle with chocolate syrup. Top with the chocolate vodka, bananas, your favorite nuts, and whipped cream. Garnish with a cherry.

ALCOHOL CONTENT:[A]

Drink Pairings: *Café Amore*	
¾ cup hot brewed black coffee 1 ounce cognac 1 ounce amaretto 1–3 tablespoons whipped cream Sliced almonds, to taste	In an Irish coffee mug combine coffee, cognac, and amaretto. Stir. Top with whipped cream. Garnish with sliced almonds.

To leprechauns, unicorns, and full bottles of Irish whiskey. May life be full of rare and wonderful things. **Author unknown**

> **Tipsy Trivia**
> The ancestor of the chocolate martini came to be in the seventeenth century when it became fashionable for Europeans to drink chocolate mixed with alcohol.

Zonked Kahlua Fudge Brownies

A bottle of wine contains more philosophy than all the books in the world.
—**LOUIS PASTEUR**

SERVES 6–8

1 box brownie mix, prepared but not cooked

¼ cup Kahlua

½ cup chopped, toasted nuts, any kind

1. Preheat the oven as instructed on mix. Add ¼ cup Kahlua to the brownie batter. Blend well. Stir in chopped nuts.
2. Bake 2–4 minutes longer than the baking time recommended in the brownie mix instructions. Cool in pan. Serve.

ALCOHOL CONTENT:

Drink Pairings: *Tawny Port*

Here's to short weeks and long weekends. **Author unknown**

> **Tipsy Trivia**
> It is said that servers in Topeka, Kansas, may not serve wine in tea cups.

Memory Lapse Banana Rum Cake

Life, alas, is very drear. Up with the glass, down with the beer!
—LOUIS UNTERMEYER

SERVES 12

Cake

1 package yellow cake mix

⅛ teaspoon baking soda

2 eggs

⅓ cup dark rum

⅓ cup olive oil

⅔ cup cream soda

1 cup banana, finely mashed

⅓ cup chopped toasted walnuts

Icing

¼ cup butter, room temperature

2 teaspoons vanilla

2 tablespoons dark rum

2 tablespoons cream

¾ teaspoon salt

3 cups powdered sugar

1. Preheat oven to 350°F. Combine all the cake ingredients (except the walnuts) in a large bowl. Mix until smooth, then fold in the nuts.
2. Pour mixture into a bundt pan. Bake for 35 minutes. Allow to cool completely.
3. For the icing, combine butter, vanilla, rum, cream, and salt. Slowly blend sugar until icing is smooth and thick. Apply icing to cake. Serve.

ALCOHOL CONTENT:

Drink Pairing: *Big Shot*	
1 ounce coconut rum 1 ounce sambuca 5 drops lime juice	Mix all ingredients in a shot glass.

However rare true love is, true friendship is rarer. **François, duc de La Rochefoucauld**

> ### Tipsy Trivia
> "Overproof" rum is 151 proof rum and is illegal in several countries. You should never drink it right from the bottle, though the occasional shot is fun.

Midnight Oil Vodka and Rum Fruit and Yogurt

Nothing makes the future look so rosy as to contemplate it through a glass of Chambertin.
—**NAPOLEON**

SERVES 4–6

16 ounces Greek-style yogurt

3 cups mixed berries (blueberries, raspberries, and strawberries)

3 tablespoons honey

2 tablespoons snipped fresh mint

3 plums, sliced

1½ tablespoons raspberry vodka

1½ tablespoons blueberry vodka

1½ tablespoons strawberry rum

¼ teaspoon salt

Walnuts (optional)

1. Mix all ingredients (except walnuts) in a bowl. Divide evenly into individual bowls. Sprinkle each serving with walnuts if desired.

ALCOHOL CONTENT:

Drink Pairing: *Theater Coffee*	
½ ounce Baileys Irish cream ½ ounce crème de cacao, white 1 cup brewed hot coffee 1 dash crème de cacao, dark 1 dash Frangelico Few tablespoons whipped cream, for garnish 1 whole cinnamon stick, for garnish	Add Irish cream and white crème de cacao to a coffee mug. Fill with coffee, but leave room for a dash of dark crème de cacao and a dash of Frangelico. Top with whipped cream and add a cinnamon stick.

Bring me a bowl of coffee before I turn into a goat.
Johann Sebastian Bach

> **Tipsy Trivia**
> In the United States, liquor laws require vodka to be distilled so that it's a neutral liquor, with no distinctive flavor. That doesn't stop liquor companies from dressing it up with everything from lemon to blueberry flavoring. Try them all!

Light My Fire Double Chocolate Ice Cream with Coconut Vodka

Ice cream is exquisite—what a pity it isn't illegal.
— **VOLTAIRE**

SERVES 1

1 to 2 scoops double chocolate ice cream

1 tablespoon coconut vodka

1 palm full of toasted nuts, your choice

1. Scoop ice cream into a bowl. Pour vodka on top and sprinkle with toasted nuts.

ALCOHOL CONTENT:

Drink Pairing: *Chocolate Martini*	
1 shaker of ice 2 ounces vodka ½ ounce crème de cacao	Place ice into a shaker and add ingredients. Shake well. Strain into a martini glass.

Go confidently in the direction of your dreams. Live the life you have imagined. **Henry David Thoreau**

Shaken not Stirred
A shaken martini has a slightly different taste than a stirred martini because the ice breaks up and adds more water to the drink.

Dream World Whiskey Pecan Pie

I never drink anything stronger than gin before breakfast.

—W. C. FIELDS

SERVES 8

1 unbaked 9" graham cracker pie shell

3 large eggs

3 tablespoons cinnamon whiskey

¾ cup dark corn syrup

¾ cup dark brown sugar

1 teaspoon apple cider vinegar

½ teaspoon cinnamon

½ teaspoon salt

¼ cup butter

1½ cups toasted pecans, chopped

1. Preheat oven to 425°F.
2. Prebake the crust in the oven for 12 minutes or until golden brown. Remove the crust from the oven and cool to room temperature.
3. Reduce oven temperature to 325°F.
4. In a medium-sized bowl, whisk together the eggs, whiskey, corn syrup, brown sugar, vinegar, cinnamon, and salt until well-combined.
5. In a saucepan over medium-low heat, melt butter. Whisk the egg mixture into the melted butter (still over medium heat). Keep whisking until the mixture starts bubbling.
6. Scatter the toasted pecans into the bottom of the cooled crust. Pour the hot mixture over the pecans. Place gently into the oven and cook for 35 minutes. Remove from the oven and cool for at least 3 hours to let set before cutting.

ALCOHOL CONTENT:

Drink Pairing: *Irish coffee*	
2 teaspoons sugar 6–8 ounces hot brewed coffee 1½ ounces Irish whiskey 1–3 tablespoons whipped cream, sweetened if desired	In a coffee mug add all ingredients except the whipped cream. Stir. Put whipped cream on top.

Here's to alcohol, the cause of—and solution to—all life's problems.
Homer Simpson

Mixology Cupcakes

I never drink water; that is the stuff that rusts pipes.

—W. C. FIELDS

MAKES 24

White cupcake batter:

¾ cup butter

1½ cups sugar

3 eggs

2 teaspoons vanilla extract

2¼ cups all-purpose flour

2¾ teaspoons baking powder

¾ cup milk

½–1½ teaspoons cinnamon whiskey

½–1½ teaspoons peach tea vodka

½–1½ teaspoons Long Island iced tea
vodka

½–1½ teaspoons ginger vodka

½–1½ teaspoons orange vodka

½–1½ teaspoons blackberry schnapps

½–1½ teaspoons gin

1. Preheat oven to 350°F. Line a cupcake pan with cupcake liners.
2. Using a mixer, cream together butter and sugar. Add eggs and vanilla and beat until mixed. Mix in flour and baking powder. Add milk and mix until the batter is smooth.
3. Fill each cupcake liner approximately ¾ full of white cupcake batter.
4. Pour ½ teaspoon of a different flavor of alcohol into each batter-filled cupcake liner. Gently mix into batter using a skewer or small spoon.
5. Bake for 20 minutes. Cool, then frost and serve.

ALCOHOL CONTENT:

Drink Pairing: *Tawny Port*

To aqua vitae and habeas corpus. May we get out of trouble as fast as we get into it. **Author unknown**

> **Roll out the Barrel**
> Tawny ports are ports that have been aged in wooden barrels, as opposed to bottle aged ports such as ruby ports. Tawny ports improve with age.

Nightcap Grand Marnier—Chocolate Mousse Pie

The problem with some people is that when they aren't drunk, they're sober.
—**WILLIAM BUTLER YEATS**

SERVES 8

6 ounces semi sweet chocolate

¼ cup Grand Marnier

Few salt grains

2½ cups whipping cream

½ cup sugar

1 cookie crumb pie crust

Whipped cream, for garnish

Chocolate shaving, for garnish

1. Melt chocolate in a large double boiler. Whisk in Grand Marnier and salt. Remove from heat and let cool to room temperature.
2. In another bowl, beat whipping cream while adding sugar a tablespoon at a time until soft peaks form. Gently fold the whipped cream into the chocolate mixture.
3. Spoon into the pie crust and chill. Garnish with whipped cream and chocolate savings if desired.

ALCOHOL CONTENT:

Drink Pairing: *Orange Cappuccino*	
2 ounces Grand Marnier 6 ounces brewed hot coffee 2 ounces whipped cream Kahlua (drizzle)	In a coffee mug, add Grand Marnier and coffee. Top with whipped cream and drizzle Kahlua over the whipped cream.

When one is sober the bad can appeal. When one has taken a drink, one knows what is real. **Johann Wolfgang von Goethe**

> **Tipsy Trivia**
> **Grand Marnier was invented in 1880 by Louis-Alexandre Marnier-Lapostolle. It combines fine cognac with orange flavors.**

Tie-One-On Red Velvet Brandy Cake

The water was not fit to drink. To make it palatable, we had to add whiskey. By diligent effort, I learned to like it.

—WINSTON CHURCHILL

SERVES 12

2½ cups all-purpose flour

1½ cups sugar

1 tablespoon cocoa powder

1 teaspoon baking soda

1 teaspoon salt

2 eggs

1 cup buttermilk

1½ cups oil

1 tablespoon vinegar

1 teaspoon vanilla

2 ounces red food coloring

Frosting

8 tablespoons butter

2 cups powdered sugar

¼ teaspoon salt

2 tablespoons brandy

1. Preheat oven to 350°F.
2. In a medium-sized bowl, combine flour, sugar, cocoa powder, baking soda, and salt.
3. In a mixer beat eggs, buttermilk, oil, vinegar, vanilla, and food coloring. Add dry ingredients to the mixer and beat on low until thoroughly mixed.
4. Pour batter into a greased, floured 9" × 13" baking pan. Bake for 25–30 minutes.
5. Let cake cool completely.
6. In a bowl, beat butter, sugar, and salt together until you have a creamy consistency. Mix in brandy.
7. Spread brandy frosting over the cake. Serve.

ALCOHOL CONTENT:

Drink Pairing: *Coffee Alexander*	
2 ounces brandy 6 ounces coffee 2 ounces whipped cream Drizzle of Chambord	In a coffee mug, add brandy and coffee. Top with whipped cream. Drizzle Chambord over the whipped cream.

To marriage. We married people cry at weddings because we know what's coming. They are tears of joy. **Author unknown**

Tipsy Trivia
Cambodia wins the prize with the world's fuzziest brandy. Tarantula brandy is made from rice liquor and dead tarantulas.

Happy Hour Buttered-Rum Apple Crisp

Among the expected glories of the Constitution, next to the abolition of slavery was that of rum.
—GEORGE CLYMER

SERVES 10

Filling

6 large Granny Smith apples, peeled and sliced

1 lemon (for zest and spritzing apples)

1 teaspoon apple cider vinegar

1 cup sugar

½ teaspoon salt

¼ cup dark rum

4 tablespoons butter

1 teaspoon cinnamon

½ teaspoon nutmeg, freshly ground

Topping

1 cup oatmeal

¾ cup all-purpose flour

¾ cup brown sugar

1 teaspoon cinnamon

½ teaspoon salt

8 tablespoons butter, frozen

¼ cup walnuts, chopped and toasted

1. Preheat oven to 350°F.
2. Grease a 9" × 13" baking pan.
3. Place apples in a bowl. Grate lemon zest over them. Spritz with lemon juice. Add the apple cider vinegar and toss the apples to distribute the vinegar. Put apples in the greased baking pan.
4. In a saucepan, warm the butter along with the remaining filling ingredients. When the mixture is smooth and homogenous, pour evenly over the apples.
5. In another bowl, combine oatmeal, flour, sugar, cinnamon, and salt. Using a box grater, grate frozen butter over dry mixture. With your fingers, rub the mixture until it's combined and crumbly. Toss in the walnuts. Spread topping evenly over the apples.
6. Bake for 40 minutes or until filling bubbles and topping is crisp.

ALCOHOL CONTENT:[A][A][A][A][A]

Drink Pairing: *Jamaican coffee*	
¾ ounce rum 1 cup brewed coffee 2 tablespoons whipped cream	In a coffee glass, combine rum and coffee. Stir. Add whipped cream if desired.

To my dog: loyal, faithful, and free of thumbs. He never drinks my rum.
Author unknown

> **Tipsy Trivia**
> Other names for rum have included kill-devil, Barbados water, pirate drink, demon water, and Nelson's blood.

Raise Your Glass to Support!

High as a Kite Chocolate Cake with Maple-Bourbon Frosting

Moderation is a fatal thing—nothing succeeds like excess.
—**OSCAR WILDE**

SERVES 12

Chocolate cake

1½ cups all-purpose flour

¾ cup sugar

¼ teaspoon cinnamon

3 tablespoons unsweetened cocoa

1 teaspoon baking soda

1 teaspoon baking powder

¼ cup vegetable oil

1 teaspoon vanilla

1 teaspoon cider vinegar

1 cup warm water

Frosting

1 cup butter

8 ounces cream cheese

3 tablespoons bourbon

2 tablespoons maple syrup

4 cups powdered sugar

1. Preheat oven to 350°F.
2. In a round 8" baking dish mix together flour, sugar, cinnamon, cocoa, baking soda, and baking powder. Make 3 holes in the mixture. Pour oil into one hole, vanilla into another hole, and vinegar into the third hole. Add warm water and mix until blended.
3. Bake for 25–35 minutes. Let baked cake cool completely.
4. In a bowl, beat butter and cream cheese until creamy. Add bourbon and maple syrup. Slowly add powdered sugar. Adjust frosting with powdered sugar or maple syrup, as needed, for desired consistency.
5. Spread frosting evenly over cooled cake.

ALCOHOL CONTENT:

Drink Pairing: *Kahlua and Cream*	
2 ounces Kahlua 1–2 cups ice 2 ounces milk or cream	Add Kahlua to an old-fashioned glass filled with ice. Fill with milk or cream. Stir.

To my computer. Without it I wouldn't drink nearly enough.
Author unknown

Cosmopolitan Vodka Root Beer Float

I'm not a heavy drinker; I can sometimes go for hours without touching a drop.
—**NOEL COWARD**

SERVES 1

1–2 scoops vanilla ice cream

1 tablespoon vanilla vodka

1 bottle root beer

1. Put 1 or 2 scoops of vanilla ice cream in a glass. Pour vanilla vodka on top. Carefully pour root beer into the glass, to reduce foaming and to keep from overflowing.

ALCOHOL CONTENT:

Drink Pairing: *Cookie Coffee*	
1 ounce crème de menthe 1 ounce Kahlua 6 ounces coffee 1 tablespoon sugar (optional) 2 ounces whipped cream Pinch of cocoa (optional)	In a coffee cup, combine crème de menthe, Kahlua, and coffee. If you'd like the drink sweeter, add the sugar. Stir. Top with whipped cream. Dust with cocoa.

To friendship, joy, ice cream, and the sweet things in life.
Author unknown

> **Tipsy Trivia**
> It takes seven years to produce a bottle of Kahlua.

Hurricane Mango Rum Vanilla Icing and Yellow Cake

The best place to drink beer is at home. Or on a river bank, if the fish don't bother you.
—**AMERICAN FOLK SAYING**

SERVES 5–6

1 box yellow cake mix, prepared and baked

1 package vanilla frosting

1 shot mango rum

1. Let baked cake cool.
2. In a bowl, mix frosting and mango rum. Add more rum as needed, for desired consistency. Spread frosting evenly over the cake.

ALCOHOL CONTENT:

Drink Pairing: *Espresso Vodka Coffee*	
1 ounce espresso vodka 1 ounce whipped vodka 1 cup brewed coffee 2 tablespoons whipped cream	In a coffee glass add vodkas and coffee. Stir. Add whipped cream if desired.

May the road rise up to meet you, may the wind be ever at your back. May the sun shine warm upon your face and the rain fall softly on your fields. And until we meet again, may God hold you in the hollow of his hand.
Irish blessing

Tipsy Trivia
A man of the people! Franklin D. Roosevelt was elected President of the United States in 1932 on a pledge to end national Prohibition.

INDEX

INDEX OF DRINKS FOR DRINK PAIRING

ABOUT THE AUTHORS

We wrote this book for you to enjoy cooking, drinking, and laughter! These experiences are found in special moments with yourself and other people. We have learned to seize the moments of life and we want to share that with you. You can never squeeze too many wonderful moments of genuine laughter and joy out of a lifetime!

Stacy enjoys finding some of these moments while at the beach chilling out with a drink, or surfing, rafting, and moments of taking in great art, while Sherri loves the adventure of travel and taking photographs of the places she visits. Stacy and Sherri love spending time with friends and family laughing, cooking, drinking, and making fun memories. Sherri loves to take photographs, make wine and beer, and go on adventure travel trips. She supports causes with animals and children. Laughter is a must!

Stacy loves anything to do with the ocean, art, music, and of course great food and drinks! She supports causes such as malaria research and animal rights. Finding moments of laughter are a given!

Enjoy each day and find as much laughter and connection with life and people as you can.

Visit us at *www.nevercooksober.com*.

the hungry Editor

Foodies Unite!

Bring your appetite and follow The Hungry Editor who really loves to eat. She'll be discussing (and drooling over) all things low-fat and full-fat, local and fresh, canned and frozen, highbrow and lowbrow. . .

When it comes to good eats, The Hungry Editor (and her tastebuds) do not discriminate!

It's a Feeding Frenzy—dig in!

Sign up for our newsletter at

www.adamsmedia.com/blog/cooking

and download our free **Top Ten Gourmet Meals for $7** recipes!

Made in the USA
San Bernardino, CA
03 February 2016